Mabel's War

Mabel's War

LOVE AND HOPE
BEYOND THE BLITZ

MABEL HEWITT
AS TOLD BY BARBARA JONES

Young love, arm-in-arm along the prom at Whitley Bay, 1947.

Praise for *Mabel's War*

Mabel's War is not just a lively, fascinating memoir of everyday reality in one of Britain's key wartime industrial cities – and most notorious of the Luftwaffe's targets – but a timely and chillingly stark reminder of the hardships and miseries of working-class life before the creation of the modern welfare state.

Frederick Taylor
war historian

It's a great read – and very moving. I didn't expect to be reading the book from cover to cover in such a short time but I was unable to put it down for more than a few minutes. Many thanks for a fascinating book.

Rev. William Howard
Secretary of The Friends of Coventry Cathedral

I haven't read anything so viscerally direct about wartime conditions. The extreme hardships bring out Mabel's feisty nature. I find the detail fascinating and I learned some things I didn't really know. The simple and direct writing style makes it seem as though it's all just happened and it's told with such clarity that its impact is immediate.

Herry Lawford
step-grandson of Coventry industrialist and philanthropist Sir Alfred Herbert

Cover illustrations: Mabel in her St John Ambulance Brigade uniform;
Mabel and John on their wedding day; bomb damage in Coventry
(Mirrorpix/Alamy)

First published 2023

The History Press
97 St George's Place, Cheltenham,
Gloucestershire, GL50 3QB
www.thehistorypress.co.uk

British Library Cataloguing in Publication Data.
A catalogue record for this book is available from the British Library.

ISBN 978 1 80399 119 1

Typesetting and origination by The History Press
Printed and bound in Great Britain by TJ Books Limited, Padstow, Cornwall.

Trees for Life

Contents

Author's Notes

by Barbara Jones

All wars devastate the lives of ordinary people. Death and glory linger on the battlefields while many millions at home suffer the pain of fear, anxiety and dread. As a war reporter, I have witnessed a great deal of anguish in the aftermath of conflicts in Afghanistan, Iraq and Libya, always conscious of how the Second World War blighted an entire generation in our own country where bombs rained down on defenceless towns and cities.

Few people are still alive to recall those times and 93-year-old Mabel Hewitt stands tall among them as a spirited eloquent eyewitness to one of the worst-ever attacks on civilians and their homes.

She endeared herself to millions when she appeared on BBC TV in a commemorative programme and talked movingly of her night in a bomb shelter during the terrible Coventry Blitz in November 1940. A reviewer for *The Times* newspaper called her 'formidably likeable'. Mabel's family asked me to work with her on producing her life story. It was inspiring, enriching, a revelation.

In a rare lifetime that spans the struggle of 1930s Britain, the onset of a cruel war and childhood memories of her city reduced to rubble in the Blitz, Mabel has a treasure-trove of wisdom she is ready to share. Her earliest memories are of a crowded house in Coventry's city suburbs with her six siblings, parents, grandmother and an uncle. Her brutally strict father ruled the household; her mother was completely cowed. Mabel remembers the fear, and the pervasive cold.

She knew even then that life could and should be better than this. Nothing would stop her seeking that out. She began to develop a determined streak that saw her survive poverty, deprivation and worse. Mabel lived through terrible times. She believes that some of today's children, in their own way, are also living through terrible times. She wants them to know that life can be better. She is a strong, determined woman who wants to inspire others through her personal example. That is why she is telling this story.

In the 1930s, there was no welfare state, no child benefit or help for the poor. The threat of the workhouse was ever present. Mabel remembers children coming to her school with no shoes. It was a life of make-do-and-mend. She was 10 when Britain found itself at war with Germany. Mabel was among the bewildered children sent to strangers' homes in the countryside to save them from the anticipated bombing onslaught.

In the chaos of the government's rushed evacuation programme, she was separated from her siblings and billeted with a family whose home life was actually harder than her own. There was no running water, just a standpipe in the yard serving several families. Her foster parents had a newborn baby who cried day and night. There was no heating, no electricity and a 'thunderbox' toilet in an outhouse. Mabel shivered miserably through the nights on an old camp bed on the landing. But worse was to come. The man of the house invited her into his bed 'to get warm' and terrified her with his advances.

She packed her cardboard suitcase and left. Mabel had found the inner strength which would see her through many tribulations as wartime bombings escalated and her city became a crucial target.

The notorious attack of 14 November 1940, when Coventry was set ablaze in Britain's longest night of German bombing raids, is etched into her memory. Mabel was hiding in the family's Anderson shelter from where she witnessed the sights and sounds of a bombardment which horrified the world. The city's medieval cathedral, fire-bombed into rubble and ashes, was at the heart of an extraordinary campaign of reconciliation and forgiveness just a few days later.

Mabel was beginning to learn about the healing power of forgiveness alongside the need to survive evil and overcome it. She was to learn assertiveness in the workplace when she left school at 14 and was assigned a lowly job in a local munitions factory. Determination won her a different career path. She wants today's youth to know they can be assertive too.

The turning point in her young life of hardship and sorrows was when she found the man who would be her husband and her rock. Love and hope, Mabel believes, are crucial. She found herself in a warm, loving family with John Hewitt and his kind parents. Together they created their own close and happy family. She lost John too soon; he died at 56. It was family and friends, and Mabel's determined cheerfulness and optimism, which saw her through.

Later she suffered a devastating illness of her own, and spent six years in treatment for bladder cancer. At 88, she received the all-clear.

Today, at 93, Mabel is an inspiration to those around her. Loved by three generations of her own family, she has a unique place in her local community with loyal friends and neighbours. Content with modest pleasures – a pretty garden, a comfortable home adapted to her mobility needs, reading and listening to music – she looks back on a life well lived and struggles overcome.

Mabel takes a keen interest in today's young people and their struggles. She wants them to know they can also find inner strength and achieve a better life. Mabel's Enterprise, a Community Interest Company (CIC) set up by her grandson Matthew in her name, aims to inspire young people. It is her way of reaching out to them.

Barbara Jones,
Foreign Correspondent

1

Born in Troubled Times

Looking back, I can see that the sad shadows of war darkened the whole of my young life. The legacy of horrendous suffering and sacrifice in the First World War was there from the day I was born. My father, strong and wiry, was a cold-hearted frightening presence to me as a small child and that fear pervaded our household. His whip-handled cane stood in the corner, ready to be snatched up and used to threaten us for any minor transgression. His old widowed mother, my Granny, lived with us in the city suburb of Holbrooks, in Coventry, and shared a bedroom with me and my sisters. We thought of her as a witch, always dressed in black, with a temper to match.

Today I understand that my father Ben Goodwin, serving as a farrier for four long years in the horse artillery at Ypres, was undoubtedly scarred by the sights and sounds of that muddy wartime hell. They say that 368,000 horses served alongside soldiers on the Western Front, holding back the

German army as it tried to fight its way through to reach the ports of Dunkirk and Calais. My father cared for horses that pulled the supply wagons carrying ammunition to the front line. Sometimes they returned carrying the wounded and dead. Always in the wintry mud. Heavy draught horses pulled artillery guns; others were ridden to take messages to the front or carry out reconnaissance. My father's skills as a farrier were crucial. He once had a bad fall from a horse, getting his foot caught in the stirrup as the animal moved ahead, breaking his ankle. He had a lifelong limp.

In the first Battle of Ypres, in October 1914, horses were often swamped with mud and died on the battlefield. They sometimes became tangled in the enemy's barbed wire and had to be shot. They suffered from fatigue, and terrible diseases like mange. The front line was terrifying for horses and men alike with its noise and chaos. My father never spoke of the horrors he had witnessed. My gradual realisation of their effect on him has taken many years. All I knew in my childhood was that there was no love or laughter or fun, or even a conversation, to be had with my father. He worked slavishly to keep us out of the workhouse. The price we all paid was that home was an unhappy, cold place where my earliest thoughts were of finding a way out.

In 1918, my father had returned to a Britain reeling from loss and sacrifice. Many families were missing their husbands, brothers and sons. There was mass unemployment and little government help.

Records show that 35,000 men from Coventry and Warwickshire went off to fight in France, many of them never to return. Our city was an important centre for munitions manufacture; all the car and cycles companies had been converted to help the war effort.

It was, ironically, a boom time for local industry. Men left to join the army, causing a huge shortage of labour. Women started working in the munitions factories for the first time and people began flooding in from other areas. The population of Coventry went from 119,000 to 133,000 in 1914.

Food shortages began to impact local families, as imports from abroad could not get through. Sugar, lard, flour and meat were hard to find and women began to form large queues outside city shops from early in the morning. Often there would be nothing but bones with a few ragged pieces of meat for them to buy once they reached the end of the queue. Boys were sent out as 'watchers' to scour the city streets looking for shops where there were some goods to buy. For a penny or two, one of them would save a place in the queue while his friend ran back to alert a housewife that it was a good time to go shopping. The government had not brought in rationing yet and some people were hoarding food. One woman was exposed in the local press for having bought dozens of bags of flour. She kept them in the bath where they got damp and maggots grew, ruining all of it.

Families were growing hungry and desperate, and their anger turned against a government refusing to recognise their problems and continuing to reassure the country that the war would be a short one. There were protests and strikes in Coventry calling for rationing so that everyone could at least share what was available.

In 1917, there was a huge demonstration in the city centre calling for 'Equal food, Equal distribution', with protesters holding up home-made banners and chanting slogans demanding rationing. The government could not afford to ignore the people of Coventry where key parts of the war effort were concentrated. By 1918, there was rationing of sugar, meat, butter and cheese.

Families were suffering from the absence of their men folk and the constant dread of bad news coming from France. Soon the Germans started to target inland towns from the air. The Zeppelin bomber was greatly feared. People had no air-raid shelters to flee to when this giant of the skies roared into view. The Germans were proud of their advanced technology. They had carried out many raids at sea using these airship bombers. Now they were aiming at civilians. The Zeppelin was a long-range airship with a metal frame, about 150m long and 18.5m in diameter, carrying a crew of up to nineteen, with seven or eight machine guns and 1,800kg of high-explosive bombs. It was powered by motors and kept afloat, lighter than air, by impenetrable bags holding hydrogen gas. It floated like a ship at a height of about 15,000ft. British planes might reach that height but had no bullets that could penetrate the bags and ignite the hydrogen gas.

It was an engineer from Coventry who invented the tracer bullet which would eventually help to bring them down. Flamboyant racing driver and engineer, James Buckingham, well known in the Spon Street area for his eccentric inventions and collection of home-made motors, studied the structure of the gas bags. They were made of cows' intestines and had, until then, proved impervious to attempts to puncture them. Working alone, he developed an incendiary bullet which could puncture the Zeppelin's bags, ignite spontaneously and set fire to the hydrogen gas inside. The Buckingham incendiary ammunition, combined with Pomeroy and Brock explosive bullets, was being used widely in Britain's fighter aircraft machine guns by 1916, shooting down or destroying 77 of the 115 Zeppelins flown over Britain in attack raids. James Buckingham became a local and a national hero, and was awarded the Order of the British Empire at the end of the war, along with a £10,000 'thank you' from the government.

Coventry was once again at the forefront of the war effort, from its munitions factories and massive workforce to its ingenious individuals with engineering skills. The city was proud of its Zeppelin hero and a new phrase came into being. 'Doing a Buckingham' was when you achieved something fair and square. Gradually, through advances like these, Britain gained the upper hand, and by the end of the First World War the Zeppelin had been rendered ineffective. By then it had claimed more than 500 lives.

Zeppelins had flown over Coventry on only a few occasions. Navigational aids were in their infancy and the Germans seemed unable to pinpoint the city accurately. The first to fly over the city, on 31 January 1917, found it in total darkness and flew on to Staffordshire to cause major destruction with its payload. However, an 80-year-old woman in Brooklyn Road, Holbrooks – my childhood home – suffered a stroke from sheer fright that night as she saw it in the sky, and died. Later, in April 1918, a Zeppelin dropped bombs in the grounds of Whitley Abbey and on the Baginton sewage farm. It had flown a successful raid after coming in from the Norfolk coast and dropping high-explosive and incendiary bombs as it headed towards the Midlands. Anti-aircraft guns opened fire but were unable to bring it down. By almost midnight it was over the grounds of Whitley Abbey where it dropped a 300kg bomb which smashed windows. Soon afterwards, two high-explosive bombs and nine incendiaries dropped on the sewage works and surrounding countryside, killing farm animals.

My father's war in Belgium had been altogether bloodier and more calamitous. He was to come home to a city emotionally devastated by the loss of its young men's lives. There was little to celebrate in the aftermath of mustard gas attacks, devastating battles at sea and the psychological wounds of a generation. His own family home was a doss-house down by Coventry railway station. Labourers from out of town, many of them poor immigrants who had left Ireland after the famine, paid 2d a night to literally sleep on a clothes' line after a hard day's work on the railways. Homeless, it was their only option. My father's mother – my 'witch' of a Granny – rented out a room where 18–20 men would hang their arms and the top part of their bodies over a rope stretched from one end of the room to the other. Somehow, they would sleep like this, fully clothed, until five or six in the morning when the rope would be mercilessly cut. Granny wanted everyone out so she could accommodate those coming off a night shift.

There were thousands of similar common lodging houses in British cities at that time. Some were so cold that on occasions a man would be found frozen to death by the morning and would be carted off to a pauper's grave. The dossers could buy a 'penny mash' from my Granny for their breakfast before heading to work. It was a spoon of loose tea and a spoon of sugar wrapped in a small twist of newspaper. They would empty it into a billycan of hot water, add some condensed milk, and hope for sufficient nourishment to get them through the morning.

These were hard times and they made for hard people. People like my Granny and my father who seemed to know little of love or kindness. He had no notion of how to bring that into family life.

He had lost his own father at the age of 3. Immediately after the First World War, the government launched an initiative encouraging young people to marry, to start families, to regenerate the broken country. My mother, quiet and submissive, had been a Sunday School teacher before she married. She was sensitive and musical, playing the organ at church and living a devout Christian life. Her basic education, along with her ten siblings, had been at a Ragged School, one of the benevolences of the Victorian era where children from poor working-class backgrounds could attend for free. Now it was the 1920s, when the creation of a large family was seen as almost a national duty. Britain needed to replace its workforce after the devastating loss of young men in wartime. There was no family planning and, at the same time, no welfare society to give support during the sharp rise in birth rates. My mother had one son and six daughters; I was the middle one, born in May 1929.

It was my mother's kindness that saw us through the bleak early years of our childhood, praying with us each night before bed and saving us from the worst of our father's wrath. We used to say the Lord's Prayer and then a prayer of her own asking God to keep us safe through the night. Three of my sisters shared a bedroom with me, Granny in her own bed in the same room. Every sound would carry downstairs from the wooden floorboards. We had no rugs or carpets. We learned to keep perfectly silent once we had been sent to bed or there would be the whoosh of the cane as my father ascended the stairs. The slightest hint of chatter and he would enter the room, laying the cane firmly down on the bed as a warning of more to come if we continued.

Granny and my father's brother, Uncle Phil, lived with us throughout my childhood. Their only alternative had been the workhouse in Gulson Road where hundreds of paupers were accommodated. A red-brick edifice which later became a hospital and is today the engineering faculty of Coventry University, it was a constant menacing presence in the 1930s. A silk mill operated inside the workhouse, using penniless men, women and children as its labourers. Nine-year-old children would receive the same pay as adults – they were allowed to keep one penny out of every shilling they earned in a ten-hour day, six days a week. The location was a byword for destitution in Coventry. A man offered a poorly paid job would know: 'It's this or Gulson Road.'

Granny had become too old and infirm to run the doss-house any longer. My Uncle Phil, in his twenties, also needed a home. He was an amiable presence, good fun and kind to me and my sisters. I remember him giving me a ride on the handlebars of his bicycle, and often offering a handful of sweets or a penny. But Granny was nothing less than a tyrant who could barely tolerate our existence. There were sharp words and smacks, and one day I saw her throw a full

Sadly, although he did manage to keep us safely housed, clothed and fed, he had no notion of paternal love.

Once at school, I came to realise that although there were many local families better off than us, we had a sort of status as my father was 'in business' and was never out of work or penniless. At home, the penny-pinching was endless. We had no electric light to see our way upstairs to bed. We carried candles. The electricity meter took coins and these were carefully regulated. If the meter ran out, the lights would go out without warning. If someone came to the door looking for cheap furniture to buy, my father would invite them to look around our own home. He once actually sold the chair I was sitting on at the table during a meal. The expression 'where there's muck there's brass' summed up his attitude. My mother often cooked over the open fire to save money. It was kept alight with wood from old furniture. My father would often find broken or old, useless chairs, tables or cupboards in the houses he was clearing. He sawed them up in the yard and there was a constant supply for the fire.

On Sundays we would have a roast joint of meat cooked in a tin oven at the side of the fire, a delicious treat. My sisters and I took turns to do the household chores, including the trip to the butcher's shop to fetch the Sunday roast. This was our contribution to family life, we were told, and there was no reward. There was no such thing as pocket money in our house. I learnt to earn some pennies by doing errands for neighbours. I was always careful with the proceeds. Later, when my school joined the National Savings Scheme, I would deposit a shilling into my account every Monday morning and proudly stick the stamps into my savings card.

Unusually, for our street in Holbrooks, we had a telephone. It had been installed high on the passageway wall where I had to take a chair to reach it if I could get there first. I would take messages from relatives of our neighbours, then keep the caller on hold while I raced up the street to fetch someone. That would earn me a penny. Sometimes a neighbour needed a prescription to be taken to the chemist. I would do that, then deliver the medicine for a penny. Or I would pick up repaired shoes from the cobbler's shop, or sweep the street in front of a corner shop.

On a Saturday morning I ran errands for Mrs Richards in the corner shop. One day she lent me her husband's bike to fetch something for her and a nasty dog chased and bit me. I followed the dog home and confronted its owner, my leg sore and bleeding. She gave me half-a-crown to keep quiet about it, knowing she could be in trouble for allowing her dog to run loose out of control. The chemist looked after my leg wound and I went home triumphant with my half-a-crown. I was learning about self-sufficiency and independence, and I had the sense to save the little money that came into my hands.

Our household chores were done before school. The worst of these was emptying the chamber pots, one from each of the three bedrooms. Our toilet was outside in a dark shed in the yard beyond the coal heap, so a chamber pot was the answer, as in many families.

I hated this job intensely and still don't like to remember it. One of my sisters and I would take our turn to carry a bucket of water upstairs. In it was disinfectant. We would empty the pots and swill them out, replacing them under the beds. We made the beds every morning, shaking up the flock mattresses to try and eliminate the lumps. Then we folded the sheets back to air the bed. We had porridge oats for breakfast with milk from a big jug my mother had filled when the milkman came round with his horse and cart. We had an apple or an orange each, whatever was in season. Then we washed up the dishes and tidied the walk-in pantry. We had no refrigerator, just a big cold concrete shelf – we called it a thrall – where my mother kept the milk and bacon or meat, with a mesh cover to keep out the flies.

Another tough job was cleaning the fire fender with Brasso, and using Silvo to remove stains from knives and forks. We had flat irons heated over the open fire, which you used two at a time. You wrapped a cloth around the handle of the hottest one then used it on the dining table covered with a sheet on top of a blanket.

While the iron in use was cooling, the second was heating up on the fire. It was precarious work for small children. Sometimes the iron was too hot and scorched the clothes; sometimes it scorched our hands. All of our school uniforms – blue blouse, navy-blue tunic, underwear and socks – had to be ironed. The tunics were the worst, with three pleats down the front. You could tell the poorest children at school; their tunics had no pleats. Sometimes a child would have no shoes.

In the years before the welfare state, schools like mine would have a poor box, filled with second-hand clothes and shoes for children to help themselves. There was no shame attached; families throughout our neighbourhood were suffering alike. You could tell their children by the ill-fitting clothes they wore. The shoes were worse. I was conscious of our social differences. School friends of mine who were only children, or one of just two, enjoyed homes altogether calmer and more orderly, and quieter, than mine.

I would be invited for tea and look around me curiously, wondering at the comfort and the warmth. An abiding memory of childhood is the cold and damp at home. The ice forming on the inside of the bedroom window, the pitiful inadequacy of the scratchy grey army blankets on our beds. The one hot-water bottle the three of us would squabble over when we got into bed. And the bare, scrubbed floorboards under our feet in the mornings. The only heat in the house came from the small smoky fire in the sitting room. My father never let us have coal from his precious heap in the yard; that was for customers only. Sometimes at night my sisters and I heard people creeping into the yard and helping themselves to pieces of coal, carrying them away in an old pram. We never alerted our father. I had already learnt there were people worse off than us, people who could not even light a fire for cooking or warmth. I didn't want them to get caught. The clothes we wore were mostly hand-me-downs, although my mother also somehow found time to knit for us. A worn-out sweater would be unravelled so the wool could be re-used. The hems of our school skirts were let down as we grew taller.

My memories of childhood playtime are centred on the little brook that ran next to our house and the field beside it. I climbed trees as well as any boy in the neighbourhood and often came home with cuts and bruises. I loved our dear old horse too. There must have been several down the years, to pull Dad's furniture removals cart. But I only remember Dolly, a gentle brown mare. She was huge to me but somehow I could hoist myself up on a fence and climb on her back. Together we would lumber around the field.

Most of our playtime was outside. At home, when it was too cold or rainy to go outside, we had board games we played together at the dining-room table. We had jigsaw puzzles, Ludo, noughts and crosses and snakes and ladders. My mother joined in sometimes and with her we did spelling games. My sisters and I never had dolls, but we made our own version. We would take a pillow and tie string at one end to make a head, then we 'dressed' her with some baby clothes. It is true that we knew no better; we weren't conscious of being deprived or of envying others who had real toys at home.

What I was most conscious of was that life could surely be better than this. We had to endure my father's bad temper and my mother's ever-present fatigue, and Granny's vicious loathing of us. I knew there could be a life where families were kind to one another; I had had glimpses of that at my friends' homes.

I longed for a life without constant battles and deep-felt resentments, much of it – I realise now – coming from unresolved bitter hurt, the legacy of the First World War. I decided early on that my future life would be altogether kinder, and that there would be no shouting. Shouting and clamour was part of daily life in our house, a great deal of it coming from Granny. She demanded my parents' attention continually with minor crises, and my sisters and I had often witnessed her virtually screaming at the top of the stairs.

I had experienced nothing but meanness and punishment from Granny in my early years so it was very confusing and traumatic to witness the shocking event which led to her death. It was a Monday morning, washday, and my father had got the gas boiler going. It heated up a large amount of water, which would be ladled into a tub where my mother scrubbed sheets and clothes by hand on a wooden washboard. Afterwards, the laundry would be hauled over to the big metal mangle to be squeezed through two rollers. There would be water all over the floor, and washing to be hung on the clothes' line in the yard. The whole process meant doors being left open and a cold draught coming in.

Granny was staying in the bedroom with a coal fire lit for her in the grate. She always wore a long black dress, her widow's weeds as they were known in those days. It seems a corner of her dress caught fire as she walked past the flames, and she was soon enveloped in them and ran screaming on to the landing.

My mother ran up to her with a blanket to smother the flames but the old lady beat her off, screaming all the time. I watched from downstairs, absolutely terrified. I was 5 years old, excited to hear an ambulance roaring up the road with sirens blaring and keeping out of the way of the burly men who carried Granny out on a stretcher. They told me she died in the ambulance on the way to hospital, a visceral and dramatic end to a terribly unhappy life.

I wanted to cry but I couldn't. I never cried as a child; I had somehow built up resilience. Granny had been a tyrant, nothing less, and I had been very afraid of her. Now my quiet acceptance of the situation was seen as good behaviour, so I was singled out as the only child of the family to attend the funeral. Mrs Barnett, the lady next door but one, made a black dress for me to wear. When we got to St Luke's Church it was absolutely packed, I remember.

The community in St Luke's Road was close, everyone knowing everyone else. In those days, families grew up in one house and didn't move away. When sons and daughters married, they often moved in with the parents. So a very large crowd turned out to pay their respects. It was the biggest single thing to have happened in my life.

It was 1935 and many well-informed people were aware there could be another world war looming. Aged 5 and innocent of all that, I thought I still had a whole childhood ahead of me.

2

The Make-Do-
And-Mend Years

The first time I ever felt completely happy was when I started primary school. I found a kindness there I had never experienced before. I realised the teachers were being especially kind to me, along with a few others, because they knew I came from a crowded household where money was short and all my clothes were hand-me-downs.

I was a rather quiet, serious child in the classroom and loved to learn, so I suppose that endeared me to them as well. My mother walked me to Holbrook primary school, joining other mothers and children along the way. There was a bus but the fare was a ha'penny and that was out of the question for us.

In those days, schoolteachers were unmarried. Education was looked on as a vocation, too important to be combined with the distractions of running a home and family. My favourite was Miss Bird, a tall lady with a manly haircut –

we used to call it an Eton crop – who arrived at school on an old-fashioned bike with her books in a basket on the front. She was strict, but there were rewards for good behaviour and I was often treated to a dolly mixture out of the little tin on her desk. We would start the morning in the playground with hopscotch and other games, then a fierce whistle would blow and we immediately stopped talking and formed into lines to go inside.

There was a hymn to start the day, with a teacher playing the piano on stage and another conducting us. We formed another orderly file to go into class. We learned our times tables by rote and there was absolutely no talking in class. There were no school dinners in those days so we went home at lunchtime. At our house we had toast or a bully beef or cheese sandwich and a hot drink. Sometimes there were eggs from the chickens we kept in the yard.

I was proud to move up to Holbrook junior school, in the same location, and by this time I was walking the fifteen-minute journey to and from home, catching up with schoolfriends along the way. I loved school; it was the one place where I felt I really mattered. I would try to get there early to help keep the cloakroom tidy when girls turned up with their coats and scarves and gloves. I helped to keep to a strict regime of tidiness and my reward was to be made cloakroom monitor, then class prefect. The discipline was extreme. A cane stood in the corner of each classroom and would be used frequently. The worst offences were talking in class and failing to concentrate.

If the teacher heard someone talking while she had her back to us, working on the blackboard, she would swivel round and hurl the blackboard rubber at the head of the guilty party. That really hurt. Similarly, a swish of the cane on a tender outstretched hand was excruciatingly painful.

A major offence would be failing to listen fully when the teacher was reading to us. She would stop suddenly during a passage of *Jane Eyre* or a similar classic and tell one of us to read the next sentence. We had to prove we were following every word. Offences could be minor ones – getting the tenses wrong in a composition for example. I remember a dozen girls standing in a line and holding their hands out for the punishment. They had mixed up 'was' and 'were' and they weren't going to get away with it. One of them, Audrey, grabbed the cane as it came down hard and headed out of the classroom with it. She ran out of school and across the road to her house. The rest of us sat there spellbound as her mother appeared outside, clearly furious, and stormed across the lawn – an offence in itself – to enter the classroom brandishing the cane and yelling at the teacher. We didn't see Audrey after that. It was a further reminder to be on best behaviour. That seemed to come easily to me and I was never once punished with the cane.

I was learning about order, something that has stayed with me all my life. At school, there was fear of punishment and there were rewards for behaving well, but most of all there was order. At home, there was fear and chaos. One of my older sisters had an unkind sense of humour and would cause trouble for me when we fell out. My father used to keep the soot from his chimney-sweeping jobs in a shed in the yard. He would sell it a bucket at a time to people for their gardens. It was greasy, smelly stuff you didn't want on your clothes.

One day I made a swing from the shed door with a piece of rope. Mary wanted a ride and when I didn't instantly let her, she ran indoors to get a knife and cut the rope so I fell and landed in the soot. My mother had to strip off my clothes and stand me in the kitchen sink to scrub it off. We usually had baths once a week, taking turns to use the same water over and over again. I always tried to be first while the water was still clean. Our house had an indoor bathroom with a hot-water geyser in it. My father would spend ages getting it to light, then run a bath which was to be shared by all the children.

My brother, the eldest of us, had left to join the army and one of my sisters was working 'in service', living in at her employer's big house. So there were five of us at home by then, along with Uncle Phil and my parents. The bath was indoors, but as the toilet was outside and there was no light, my sisters and I hated going out there after dark. We used to go in pairs with one of us standing guard outside in case strangers came into the yard to steal coal. On a Saturday night after tea, my parents would walk to the Park Gate pub nearby and have a few drinks of stout. Our pet dog Spot, a little mongrel bitch, went with them.

Life had its rituals, but these never included holidays. Instead, we had days out, and these were a special treat. We had a pony and trap one summer, pulled by Dolly the horse. My father would load us children on to the back seats and sit up front to control the horse. We loved to trot along the familiar streets and out of town to the village of Corley, about 6 miles away, where my aunt and uncle lived.

Later my father bought a van for his furniture removals and on a late summer Saturday or Sunday he would drive us over to Evesham in Worcestershire for a picnic and a day at a roadside orchard. Scrumping apples and plums was a big problem in this area so the local authority had planted fruit trees at the roadside where poor families could help themselves. We parked up our van, spread out a blanket and helped ourselves to hard-boiled eggs, jam sandwiches and tinned salmon, with a flask of tea. I remember the lovely Russet apples and the golden plums, so plentiful that we could eat some with our picnic and take some home with us. Many people joined us there, some on foot, many with horses and carts.

One Christmas, I remember going into Coventry city centre to the shops with my mother. It was just her and me, getting there on the bus. The lights and the shops were the most glamorous sights I'd ever seen. We went to Woolworths and British Home Stores and Mum bought presents. I met Father Christmas and that was a treat, but it was the coloured lights that mesmerised me.

In the school holidays and at weekends, my sisters and I would run a little bit wild. Mum was always weighed down with household chores so we would take out baby Irene in her pushchair and go down to the brook to play. We climbed trees and, inevitably, fell into the brook quite often. It was shallow running water, clean and sparkling. We would take jam jars with a handle made of string and collect tadpoles and tiddlers. We made a rope swing and there was a lot of shouting and laughing as we tried to hang on as it carried us over the water. One or other of us would often go home wringing wet, Spot the dog running along beside us, having the time of her life.

Once we took the pushchair and the dog to the canalside, very much against the rules, and went off to play, leaving the pushchair and Spot tied up together to a hedge on the towpath. When we returned, Irene was at the water's edge, saved from tipping into the canal by loyal Spot who had braced herself against the pushchair. It was only many years later that we told Mum about it. I remember long hot summers and the ritual of Sunday morning service at St Luke's, dressed smartly and thinking more about Mum's roast beef to come than we did about the hymns and prayers.

Rosie grew into a little daredevil as she got older. She really paid the price for that after an ill-advised trick where she hung on to the back of Dad's van as he drove off. Kids would sometimes do that for a ride on the tailboard, jumping off before the vehicle picked up speed. But Rosie was still somehow holding on when Dad accelerated to drive up a hill away from the house. He had no idea she was clinging to the back of the van until a cyclist nearby yelled to him to stop. Rosie injured her legs badly and wore an iron leg-brace for quite a while after that to straighten her limbs. It was a common sight in those days to see children with leg-braces, often because of rickets caused by malnutrition.

At that time, we had no realisation that as early as 1935 the government was so concerned about another war with Germany that it had ordered cities like Coventry to set up Air-Raid Protection committees to prepare to keep the civilian population safe. The city council was apparently unenthusiastic, believing in pacifism and reluctant to gear up for war again. When the Air-Raid Precautions Act became law at the end of 1937, Coventry was lagging behind other cities with only 44 per cent of the required precautions in place. Two years later, in March 1939, Coventry, along with all the country's major authorities, received its sealed War Orders. The local Civil Defence Service was put under the command of the chief constable, and air-raid wardens were undergoing training alongside the Red Cross and St John Ambulance Brigade. A volunteer auxiliary fire service was set up to work with the official fire brigade, with orders to patrol neighbourhoods. My father joined them. There were plans for blackouts, and factories were painted in camouflage.

Something that reverberated badly on Coventry later when incendiary bombs began to fall was the failure to pre-pare adequate water supplies to combat the flames. We know now that there were two main reservoirs holding 20 mil-lion gallons of water each for the normal requirements of the city. The canal could be used and the River Sherbourne nearby was supplied with dams to provide extra water tanks. I remember huge water tanks being installed at the corner of some streets in our neighbourhood. But there were Home Office recommendations for the further construction of steel dams which could hold up to 200,000 gallons of water for firefighting. Coventry did not act on these. I was hardly aware of this increasing sense of urgency and was living my young life oblivious to government announcements or newspaper headlines. I had a good network of friends; I loved my schooldays and only occasionally would I hear my parents talk of troubles to come.

On a sunny Sunday morning in September 1939, on our return from the church service at St Luke's, we were told to stay quiet while my parents sat close to the wireless to hear the prime minister's speech. Neville Chamberlain was talking of slaughter in Poland. He said Britain was at war with Germany. The vague unspecified fear which had been haunting the back of my mind had suddenly become real. I was 10 years old, in a cold terror.

Our family was not one for sharing feelings and now I did not turn to my mother or father, or sisters. I fled across the road to the bridge overlooking the brook and wept inconsolably. I had a single thought – there's going to be war and fighting, and I will die.

Everything changed, and nothing changed. There was to be rationing of food and sweets and we would not see another orange or banana for several years. Black cloth was provided for every window, the street lights went off permanently, and families like ours began to build underground shelters at the back of our houses. My father paid £7 for a government kit that provided corrugated-iron sheeting to be dug 4ft into the earth in an arc, leaving 2ft clearance above ground for an entrance. It contained bunk beds to accommodate six. I remember him choosing a spot for it behind the house. But I still got dressed in that chilly bedroom each morning, had my porridge and walked to school. I loved school; it was my sanctuary away from everything. I didn't want to believe war was coming any more than those who named that strange period 'the Phoney War'. I didn't want to believe it even when they gave us all gas masks and taught us how to use them.

Two weeks after the announcement of war, we started to hear a strange new kind of radio programme. It was Lord Haw-Haw, the English traitor who was in Nazi Germany, broadcasting propaganda over the airwaves to persuade British people we should surrender.

It was a fascinating phenomenon of the Second World War. This man with a very upper-class English accent spelling out how hopeless it was for us to try and fight off the Germans. He became hugely popular as more and more people tuned in. He would start off in a very posh accent saying, 'Germany calling, Germany calling' and then entertain us with a funny, sneering and sarcastic sense of humour.

The Ministry of Information became extremely worried about his popularity; it seems that one out of six adults in Britain were listening to him regularly. Children like us listened to him too. His broadcasts were different from anything else we heard. To us he sounded funny and witty. The government was sufficiently worried to carry out a survey. People told them: 'He sounds nice, genuine. It makes you think there might be something in what he's saying.'

Haw-Haw, who was revealed to be William Joyce, a senior member of the British Union of Fascists who had become a naturalised German citizen, reached 50 per cent of British people in the first eight months of the war. He was a novelty, and was cleverly trying to discourage and demoralise the British people so they would press the government to make a peace deal with the Germans that would keep the Nazis in power. Lord Haw-Haw continued to broadcast until the night of 30 April 1945, when he signed off: 'Heil Hitler and farewell.' Adolf Hitler committed suicide a few hours later. Joyce wasn't captured until the end of the war when British soldiers found him in northern Germany and brought him back to be hanged in Wandsworth Prison in January 1946 for treason.

It seemed harmless to be tuning into his nightly broadcasts at a time when we had not seen or heard a single bomb and people were fed up with being expected to stay on high alert and suffer food shortages. No one wanted another war. We were just in a limbo that went on and on. Looking back, the Phoney War was a period of peace combined with a sense of fatalism. There was a feeling of 'Eat, drink and be merry, for tomorrow we die' about it.

3

Evacuation:
A Painful Ordeal

Christmas 1939, as always, was wonderful. The house was full of people; family and friends who lived nearby would call with bottles of home-made wine and cakes. We had bought a cockerel from a farm outside town and got busy plucking it and drawing it, an unpleasant task but all part of the annual ritual. The front parlour, rarely used, with its green velour sofa and its dark-brown sideboard and stuffed armchairs, was open to all. We sat and opened our Christmas stockings, finding nuts and sweets, colouring books and crayons, little celluloid dolls and games of dominoes. We had a real Christmas tree with paper decorations we loved to unpack from the previous year.

But there had been talk of millions of children being sent away from their homes to places of safety in the countryside and those rumours were getting louder by the New Year of 1940. More than a million children had already been sent out of London, off to rural areas where, the government was telling families in propaganda headlines, they would be safe and happy. Some parents had been reluctant to send their children to an unknown destination to be taken in by complete strangers.

A nationwide publicity campaign urged them to register their children for evacuation. Bizarrely, the evacuation plan was named Operation Pied Piper, a reference to the menacing German folktale in which children are lured to their peril. As the railway stations of London thronged with crowds of school groups and weeping mothers, the Parliamentary Secretary to the Minister of Health, Violet Horseburgh, saw some of them off, telling women: 'Cheer up. Your children are going to have a happy holiday, don't worry.'

In Coventry, only a fifth of parents had registered their children for evacuation, and only a third of that number turned up on 4 September, the day after war was declared. Parents were having misgivings, and who could blame them? The truth is that although the send-offs, usually groups of children with their school teachers, were more or less organised at bus, coach and railway stations, the receiving end of this mass migration was chaotic in many cases.

My sisters and I weren't sent away with the first wave so we were lucky to have Christmas at home. But by spring 1940 there were grave forebodings of imminent German attacks and my mother told us we were going away for a while, just to be safe. Minister of Health Malcolm MacDonald had announced in a broadcast on 30 May that there was going to be a second wave of evacuations due to expectation that bombing would start soon. 'That time may be very near,' he said. 'The government feel that the risk of that bombing is so real that it is right to make as complete as possible now the plans for this evacuation.' His broadcast was frightening and sinister. He continued:

On this occasion war is going to be brought right home to this island. The same indiscriminate, savage air attacks on our industrial cities and towns as have been experienced by our Allies on the Continent must be expected. The enemy certainly will not desist from that in our case; rather he will endeavour to strike us most hard and most mortally, for here in this island is one of the decisive, the indomitable centres of resistance to his will.

The formal language struck fear into the heart of every man, woman and child listening to the wireless. But when my sisters and I heard that we would be going away, all we could think of in our excitement was the unexpected holiday ahead of us. We were given a small cardboard suitcase each and packed a change of underwear, our nighties, a pair of plimsolls, a toothbrush, comb, towel and handkerchiefs. We wore our best clothes: jumpers and skirts and polished black shoes and socks. We each carried a gas mask. We printed our names carefully on to paper labels and these were pinned to our gaberdine coats. I discovered later that many children had got lost or gone missing in the chaos of evacuations in London and other big cities.

For all of us one thing was true: we were among millions of children being sent out to unknown destinations where 'foster parents' who had not been screened or vetted would be receiving 10s 6d a week for each of us, leading in many cases to unknown trauma and suffering for subsequent decades. David Prest, the producer of *Evacuation: The True Story*, a five-part series for BBC Radio 4, has called the initiative 'a typically British wartime shambles. Hundreds of children arriving in the wrong area with insufficient rations and more worryingly, not enough homes to put them in.'

It seems that middle-class and well-off families, fearful of taking in rough urchins from inner cities, had notified the government they had no room – they were taking in relatives or friends and didn't want to be part of the mass movement. Local authorities were responsible for housing children, but it was hopelessly amateurish, with town hall employees promoted to 'billeting officers' and tasked with finding bed spaces. In many areas, children were bundled into village halls, lined up against a wall or on the stage and made available to potential hosts who could take their pick.

One girl who, years later, told her sad story to the TimeWitness forum, part of a charitable trust formed of retired teachers and academics, described her long bus journey from London's docklands to Jericho, a suburb of Oxford. She was with her two brothers, ending up in a village hall where they were split into groups and 'dragged through the streets with billeting officers knocking on doors. We were almost the last to be picked as no one wanted three children together. I felt really unwanted.' She and one brother were left at a small house while the remaining brother went elsewhere. She said their foster parents told them plainly that they weren't wanted. Parcels and money sent by her mother were never handed over. 'I was treated like a slave, no affection at all,' she said. 'I felt my foster mother hated me. We had to see ourselves off to school and we weren't allowed in the house if she was out. I was sent out in the bitter cold to run errands. My hands chilblained and I always felt hungry.' She said the man of the house was kind to her brother and brought him toys. But, sinisterly, she was subject to 'mild sexual abuse' from him and was too afraid to tell anyone.

This 7-year-old girl's nightmare experience was one of a minority, but studies show that at least 12 per cent of evacuees suffered some sort of mental, physical or sexual abuse, and carry deep scars to this day. Of course, for many evacuees their 'holiday' in the countryside would remain a lifelong happy memory. They remember learning to cook, or to care for farm animals, and go bird-watching for the first time. But we now know that others were beaten, mis-treated and abused by families who never wanted them and were either cajoled into taking a child or did it simply for the extra money.

A leaflet sent out to householders who had offered to take unaccompanied children told them they must control and care for them as if they were their own. The payment of 10s 6d for one child or 8s 6d a week for each child if they took more than one would be made weekly in advance, through forms to be cashed at the local post office.

Emergency rations were to be supplied to cover the first forty-eight hours and householders were warned 'not to rush to the shops'. Children would have no bedding with them, and people could ask the local authority for some if necessary. Arrangements would be made for the children to continue their education and local schools might have to work in shifts. There was advice on how to keep an evacuee child 'healthy and happy' with a well-balanced diet. A leaflet describing 'specimen meals suitable for a child of school age' spelt out details for breakfast, dinner and tea. Breakfast was always weak tea or milk with porridge or other cereal, and bread and dripping or bread and butter, with an occasional egg or fried bread, herrings or haddock.

The recommended dinner was roast beef or mutton with potatoes and greens and a currant roll; or minced meat and tomatoes and potatoes followed by baked bread pudding, jam tart or boiled apricot pudding. Stewed steak and onions, boiled silverside and hotpot were all on this imaginary menu.

For tea, children should be given bread and butter, cheese and jam, or potted meat, or even baked beans. They should be fed at regular hours and given plenty of water to drink. Baths should be given as often as possible, but 'at least once a week' and 'it would be better to have a tin basin of fresh water for each child than to allow them to share a bath'. Bedroom windows should be kept open at night and it should be remembered that young children needed eleven hours sleep.

The final word of advice was that children would be in strange surroundings and might be homesick. 'You should therefore watch them carefully for the first few days.'

Wise words indeed and clearly many foster parents took that advice to heart. For others their interest peaked at the information about payments and they read no further. Either way, in hindsight, Operation Pied Piper was little short of a disaster waiting to happen to many of us and for me it was to be especially miserable.

Of course, I had no idea what was in store and as my sisters and I prepared for our adventure we were cheerful and carefree. Arriving at school that day, we piled happily on to coaches, thinking of outings to the countryside and a change of scenery. We drove down the old Roman road, Watling Street, and stopped at Wilnecote village, near Tamworth. My two sisters, Rosie and Mary, and I were about 23 miles away from home and were told to disembark. A kind lady, probably from the WVS – the Women's Voluntary Service – told us we would all be living in the village but in separate homes. My sister Mary was the lucky one; she went to a large house where the family was kind to her and bought her new clothes. Rosie went to a welcoming family in a little cottage quite near to my lodgings. But for me it was an unforgettably miserable ordeal which upsets me to this day.

I was led up a little lane between houses on the main road and brought to the doorstep of a brick cottage where a man and woman were at the entrance. There was no welcome and no smile. This young, poverty-stricken couple were living in extreme hardship. Their living room was sparsely furnished and the floor was bare stone. A coal fire was smoking in the hearth and a baby was wailing in its crib.

There was no electricity or running water and no bedroom for me. I was to sleep on an old camp bed on the landing. It was cold and draughty and damp. The woman told me I would be looking after the baby, dressing it and taking it for walks. I flatly refused, telling her, 'I don't like it here, I want my mum. I'm not stopping here.' But I had no choice. Every day, all day, the homesickness rose in me like a wave of nausea. I wasn't normally a tearful child, but I cried hot tears day and night.

There was no bathroom in the house; we had to share a standpipe outside in the yard with the neighbours. There was cold water only and, worse, the outside toilet was a 'thunderbox' shared with several families. A makeshift school had been set up in the village and I would walk there gladly just to get away from the hell of my foster home. There were overflow classrooms in the corridors to accommodate the sudden influx of new pupils. At night, it was difficult to sleep with the metal crossbars of the camp bed frame digging into my sides. Most nights I cried myself to sleep, unable to imagine an end to the bleakness.

We had been given a stamped postcard each to send to our parents, letting them know our whereabouts. That was my only contact with home for the several months I spent in Wilnecote. Government 'experts' had advised parents not to visit their children during evacuation for fear of upsetting them. Compassion seemed not to come into it. I've since learnt that among the many studies revealing the psychological damage and trauma caused to children randomly placed with wartime evacuation hosts there is a report by clinical psychologist Steven Davis, which describes the programme as 'a paedophile's charter'. He counsels former evacuees who remember the chaos of arriving unbilleted in villages where local people were invited to just 'take their pick'. Strong boys would be favoured by farmers wanting free labour and girls would often be used as virtual servants.

Others, like me, experienced worse. On a freezing cold night as I lay unhappily in my camp bed, while the woman of the household was downstairs with the baby, her husband invited me into his bed 'to get warm'. Within seconds he was making unpleasant advances which terrified and disgusted me. I had no knowledge of sexual activity, but I knew this was wrong. Like many children, I felt that somehow it had been my fault and at the same time this was bad and frightening. I flew back to my camp bed and vowed it would be my last night in this house.

In the morning, I ate breakfast in silence as usual with my foster parents. The baby continued to cry. I was leaving and no one would be able to stop me. I packed my brown cardboard suitcase and carried it with me. It was a Saturday morning so there was no school. I had made my first grown-up decision. I was doing something I believed was right and I felt strong and unstoppable. Mabel Goodwin, aged 11, was going home.

It is extraordinary now to think that I had no idea which direction would take me home. I just trudged down Watling Street, crying and angry, and after a while I began to feel better. The gods were smiling on me that day, the first time for a long time. I heard a vehicle pull up behind me and saw my father winding down the window. He was returning from a long-distance house removal job and happened to be coming home on this route, the main arterial road out of Coventry. I couldn't tell him the shameful truth, I just said I wouldn't stay there any longer and I wanted my mum. He drove to the house in Wilnecote and I watched triumphantly from the van as he knocked on the door and informed them their fostering days were over. Coming home was of course a relief. My safety from German bombardment was not the issue; my immediate need was to follow my mum from room to room to make sure I was really home for good.

I had been away for months. It was early summer 1940 and there was a tangible sense of expectation in Coventry. Rationing had begun in January along with the practice of nightly blackouts. Our many engineering industries were now all geared towards the war effort. A thousand new workers were turning up in the city every month to fill increasing job placements. Coventry had become a boom town again, mirroring the prosperity of its past as a great medieval centre of the silk ribbon and wool trades. It was a crucial centre of armament manufacturing, making the machines that would make the munitions, planes, aero engines and aircraft accessories. Workers, many of them migrants from poorer areas, were thronging the pubs and cinemas with money in their pockets. The government's Mass Observation Unit, an offshoot of the Ministry of Information, reported many individuals echoing public opinion in a strong desire to spend their money now.

My own mother had that same sense of terrible times to come. She would occasionally use up all our rations of meat, butter and sugar for dinner, saying, 'Let's have a good meal now, we might not be here tomorrow.' I was back at school, conscious of the tension, but as usual I was glad of the sense of order there. On 25 June 1940, a month after my eleventh birthday, the first bombs fell on Coventry.

The Germans had come and we knew – men, women and children – that the intention was to completely destroy us. Here in my city, where Britain's war machinery was being built, we would all of us be prime targets in our homes, our streets, our schools and even our churches.

4

Storm Clouds Gathering

The haunting wail of the air-raid sirens became a nightly ritual, a sound that quickened your pulse and shredded your nerves. I would have been home from school for a few hours, having my tea, clearing dishes and washing up, then getting into my 'siren suit' in readiness for a frightening, uncomfortable night in the Anderson shelter. My mother had ingeniously cut up some old coats and sewn them together to make a 'onesie' for each of us with a zip or buttons and a hood to keep us warm during long wakeful nights in the shelter. Mine was blue. I zipped it up and pulled up the hood, using it to muffle the terrible sounds of a bombing raid.

We watched the clock in the house until 7 p.m. came and then the inevitable wail would start up. Mum had already made a flask of tea. My sister Pat and I walked across the yard, finding our way, not speaking. Mum was ahead of us carrying 2-year-old Irene, trying to guide us in the dark. We climbed in through the tarpaulin-covered entrance, pulling the cover down behind us, squelching across duckboards that were seeping mud, and climbing into the two bunk beds, one on either side. We were frightened to death, lying there in dread.

When the first German bombs dropped near Coventry on 25 June 1940 it was in a raid 5 miles away at Ansty airfield where the RAF had a training squadron. No one was killed but for us it was a turning point. The war really was going to come that close. Two days later, a raid on Hillfields, a city suburb, killed sixteen people. On 25 August, hundreds of bombs were dropped in the city centre, injuring nineteen people and completely destroying the Rex Cinema, a glamorous venue with its Wurlitzer organ and ornate, mirrored restaurant which had been grandly opened by the mayor in 1937. The air raids seemed to be indiscriminate. The overriding thought was always: 'When will it be our turn?'

My dad was a fire-watcher and set off for the Auxiliary Fire Service each night with Spot the dog, his constant companion. All the volunteers met in a brick-built hut across the fields. During the night, he would turn up at our shelter from time to time to see if we were okay, see if we were still alive. We knew he was also going to Baginton airport, but it wasn't till long after the war that he told us he was part of a team plotting enemy aircraft. I don't know when he can have had any rest. His furniture removals and second-hand business had developed into house clearance for the unlucky families whose homes had had a direct hit. And he was still sweeping chimneys and hauling coal. My sisters and I were far from close to my dad, but it was horrifying to see him one night appearing at the entrance to the air-raid shelter wringing wet, with Spot similarly soaked to the skin and shivering. The fire-watching team had seen a parachute falling and rushed over to capture the German soldier hanging from it. It wasn't a soldier at all; it was an incendiary bomb which had exploded on impact.

These bombs were to be the new menace of the Second World War. They were metal cylinders 34.5cm long by 5cm diameter, filled with thermite. The bomb didn't explode, but on impact a needle drove the igniter into a small percussion cap, setting fire to the thermite which quickly became hot enough to melt steel. They became the Germans' weapon of choice when dropped alongside high-explosive bombs. The fires showed the target and set fire to rooftops, while the explosives destroyed the rest of the building. When they were dropped with their own parachute it was easy to mistake them for a distant human, dropping from the sky.

The blast had thrown my father and his team, and Spot, backwards into the brook. They were badly shaken and my father's greatest concern was that the bundle of cash he always kept in his back pocket had been soaked and might be worthless. All of his work ventures were cash transactions and we often saw him counting the huge roll of notes, licking his thumb as he went. That night, after the all-clear siren sounded, we went back to the house to find he had laid each green pound note, red ten-shilling note and large white five-pound note carefully on the furniture in the front parlour to dry. We were forbidden to enter that room until the money had dried out and could be collected up again.

The incendiary bombs had been assembled with all of Germany's advanced technology, guided in by their pathfinder radar and beams. At the time, the German wartime devices were far more sophisticated than Britain's and they were later to be spectacularly destructive on Coventry's worst night under bombardment. Our local Civil Defence Service was being controlled by the police and each home had strict instructions about firefighting to somehow deal with the new menace of the incendiary bombs. It was pitiful really to think of our single bucket of water, stirrup pump and a bucket of sand outside the back door. We had been instructed by government information posters on how to deal with incendiary bombs. It was a lot more complicated than a couple of buckets.

Ideally, you would need a wooden scoop, a small axe, a crowbar, torch, a wooden shovel, dark glasses, a wooden sand bucket, a stirrup pump, water tins and sand mats. The instructions were to lay the sand bucket on its back, shovel sand over the bomb, place the bucket upright, scoop the bomb into the shovel and tip it into the wooden bucket. Carry to a safe place was the rather hopeful culmination of those actions.

Alternatively, you could:

Enter the burning room on hands and knees. Open the door slowly, keeping down low to avoid smoke and flames. Take cover and direct a jet of water on to burning fabric, not the bomb itself. The person operating the stirrup pump should stay outside the room. A third person should bring more water. Never throw water on to the bomb, it will explode.

So that was an information poster we really couldn't take seriously; none of us were going to be able to do any of that.

We needed to believe that Dad and his team had the necessary training. And we wanted to believe that an incendiary bomb wouldn't come close to us. When the full impact of war arrived later in our city, we saw the death and destruction that tens of thousands of incendiary bombs could bring. The notion of an untrained family dealing with one of these evil weapons was out of the question.

The Germans were by now gearing up for full-scale destruction of factories and homes and their navigation radar was proving far superior to Britain's attempts to catch up with the technology.

Our nights were a time of terror, but when day dawned it seemed to be business as usual. Mum would often set off for the family allotment in Watery Lane, quite a walk away. She was growing potatoes, cabbages, sprouts and carrots in a community effort where neighbours shared their gardening tools and seedlings. Dad made her a crude sort of wheelbarrow out of pram wheels with a box on top and wooden handles. She would push it there and return with vegetables for a stew, or a pie when lard or butter rations permitted. She was a good, resourceful cook and there were plenty of ration coupons in our household owing to the size of the family. Meat rations would allow us a joint on Sundays and Mum would get out the big metal mincing machine on Mondays to make a meal from the leftovers. I loved the cottage pies made with leftover meat, and the delicious faggots put together with chopped onions and minced-up liver. In summer we had plums, pears and apples and she bottled these to provide puddings in the winter, along with the treacle sponge puddings and steamed jam roly-polys that still make me feel nostalgic.

Mum made custard tarts using eggs from the chickens we shared with neighbours, and occasionally she baked bread in the little oven next to the open fire. Our family shared a pig with the neighbours too, all of us feeding it with 'swill' made from household food scraps until it was ready to be slaughtered. The pork joints, chops and offal would be shared out equally among us all. We had a good table and never went without. The smell of home-baking was a treat on our return from school.

It seems extraordinary now that we lived a semblance of normal life during the war years, but it seemed to be the only way to get through it. I think it was a blessing that there was no television so we weren't seeing live footage of the reality of wartime destruction. That would have destroyed morale and made us all feel more wretched. As it was, there was a daily toll that was heartbreaking. At school, once we had heard the playground whistle, we all filed into the hall where our head teacher would address us. We stood in hushed silence as she told us the solemn news. The family of a schoolfriend losing their home after a bombing raid; the death or injury of our classmates; an outbreak of sickness like measles, mumps or whooping-cough.

I remember girls dying of sickness or suffering from polio and having to wear leg-braces. Others had rickets through malnutrition and there were regular inspections by the school nurse who came round to check for nits or eye infections. These inspections were an ordeal. I hated having to strip to my vest and knickers for an intrusive going-over by the nurse. We all got nits and lice of course and went home with a special shampoo to try to get rid of them. The smell of carbolic soap permeated the school. These early interventions were important in the days before antibiotics were available. Older people were dying from pneumonia and bronchitis.

My dad had a weak chest in his later years, the legacy of his chimney-sweeping days. He had a painful knee condition too and I remember one day we were all frightened to hear him crying out in pain when the family doctor lanced it to drain infected liquid. I was fortunate never to suffer from serious illness, but there's no doubt that the regular enemy bombardments took their toll on our mental health. At night there would be cold fear hour after hour as the unique sound of hate-filled bombing rang in our heads and shook the ground underneath us. It started with the intermittent drone of the engines – the Heinkels and the Junkers. Then the whistle and scream of bombs raining down. The thuds and the explosions. Debris falling and the anguished shouting, swearing and cursing of those in its direct path.

We had government-supplied army blankets to try to combat the cold and damp. The corrugated-iron walls around us would be running with icy condensation. And all the time we strained our ears for the sound we dreaded. The Heinkel bombers' approach was unmistakable – it was a Brummm! Brummm! Brummm! A staccato sort of noise, which I learnt later was due to the Germans having de-synchronised the engines to confuse sound detectors. As children we learnt to distinguish between the approaching sound of the Devil himself, and the one-note thrum of a British aircraft, the friendliest noise you ever longed to hear.

Before the war, my sisters and I used to stand at our bed-room window and marvel at the bright lights and activity at the dog-racing stadium in nearby Lythalls Lane. We had a grandstand view from the first floor of our house. When the blackout rules came in, the lights went out after dark and the armed forces moved in. A huge anti-aircraft gun was installed there and the tremendous booming sound of its efforts to shoot down enemy planes added to the hellish racket inside our shelter.

One night during a bad raid, my father and his fire-watcher team scaled the gates of the stadium to let the greyhounds out and give them a better chance of survival. Incendiary bombs had set the place on fire. One terrified, shivering dog turned up near the entrance to our shelter. My mum said, 'Mabel, let the poor thing in. Let him on to your bed.' I spent the rest of the night clinging to that poor bundle of skin and bones. I could feel his ribs and he shook constantly with fear. I think we comforted each other; something warm to cling on to when the sound of death was raging all around.

Many times, I felt certain I was going to die. Or worse, my mum would die. I was so frightened I literally shook with fear during those bombardments. First the unmistakable sound of approaching enemy planes, then the whistle of bombs being dropped. Earth-shaking thuds as they hit the ground, then worst of all, the explosion. The mind-blowing splintering of millions of shards of shrapnel and the accompanying ignition of incendiary bombs creating walls of flame. I heard debris falling from roofs, angry shouting and hysterical crying, dogs barking, bombs thudding and ricocheting all around us.

But the worst sound of all was of my mother praying, praying out loud for God to save us. She would say, 'God help us, oh please God help us.' She was the foundation of our young lives, providing and caring and keeping us safe. Now she was scared we would die. If she was scared, it meant our world must be coming to an end. The Germans hated us enough to bring this terror to us – innocent families trying to live decent lives. I lay there in silence, wondering who these people could be.

5

My City, Hitler's Target

On Sundays – going to a service in the morning then back again in the afternoon for Sunday School – the vicar read out the names of families who had been killed by the bombing, or lost their homes and all they possessed. I began to feel angry, lying in my cold, damp bunk bed at night, my hands over my ears, further terrified by every deafening thud from the nearby anti-aircraft guns in the stadium.

Why was God allowing this? Was there really a God who was kind and merciful? My mum, who had the kindest heart, told us often that, yes, there was a good God. 'Look around you at the trees and the sky, the clouds and rain and the birds, and nature, everything you can see,' she would say. 'God has given us all this. He doesn't deserve your anger. This war is coming to us from a man, from Hitler, not from God.' But I was angry, livid, at the enemy action visited on us every day. My intense fear had turned into intense anger. There were so many funerals processing from our church,

St Luke's. Often several members of a family we knew. My father knew all the details because of his work with the Auxiliary Fire Service.

I would hear him tell my mother in the mornings, 'The Smith family got it last night, the whole family wiped out' or 'You know the people at number 82, they got it last night. A direct hit on their air-raid shelter. Only the little boy survived and he's in a really bad way in hospital.'

Once in the shelter we heard an enemy plane shot down. We started cheering, 'Hooray, Jerry's down!' My mother wouldn't have that. There, in the misery of the shelter, bombs dropping around us and half the city in flames, she scolded us. 'Be quiet. That's nothing to cheer about. Those men are sons and husbands of families just like ours.' Years later I got to wondering if the mothers in Berlin and Dresden were thinking that when Britain's bombers were shot down over their cities.

Sometimes the bombardments would continue until 9 p.m., sometimes all night. We waited wearily for the all-clear before wending our way back to the house. It seems extraordinary now but we routinely dressed for school and set out to walk there, meeting up with friends on the way. Sometimes we would see British soldiers up ahead where the army had been called in to deal with an unexploded bomb. These were frightening situations. A German bomb would have crashed into the road, forming a huge crater, and there it sat, ready to explode and blow us all to smithereens. The soldiers would usher us away, telling us to go home. There would be no school that day. We marvelled at their discipline, the way they formed a screen for the safety of children like us and other people setting off for work. They were waiting for the bomb disposal experts and all the time at grave risk themselves.

Coventry's bombing raids created many heroes in those years. In October 1940, a Second Lieutenant Sandy Campbell from the Royal Engineers bomb disposal unit was called to an unexploded bomb at the Triumph Engineering Works in Canley, 5 miles from our home. The work had been stopped and employees and local residents evacuated. The young officer found a delayed action fuse that was impossible to remove. He lay beside the bomb as it was carried to a place of safety on a lorry, listening to the ticking so that he would be able to warn the driver to stop and escape if necessary. He got the bomb safely away and defused it. But the next day he was killed in a separate incident. Second Lieutenant Campbell was posthumously awarded the George Cross, one of several major bravery awards earned during Coventry's war years.

My sisters and I knew that our city and our homes were being targeted because Coventry was an important centre for the war effort. All the factories and engineering works that normally turned out motor cars or bicycles were now fully engaged in making munitions and planes and tanks. It was inevitable that Germany would want to destroy that. The Air Ministry had set up the Shadow Scheme in 1935, which obliged motor manufacturers to use their advanced technology to make fighter planes instead. Coventry was the heart of British motor manufacturing and was ordered to set up five 'shadow' factories which the government would fund and equip, where motor mechanics and engineers, already highly skilled and trained, would be building planes and accessories for the RAF.

New premises were built to house the production lines, usually alongside existing motor factories. The 'shadow' did not mean secrecy. It referred to people working 'in the shadow' of their normal jobs.

By the end of October 1937, shadow versions of Austin, Daimler, Humber, Standard and Rover were all in production in Coventry, making Bristol Mercury aero engines. By July 1938, the Austin factory had built a complete bomber plane and it was flown out in front of Sir Kingsley Wood, Secretary of State for Air. All this meant massive employment opportunities. The shadow factories operated twenty-four hours round, in shifts. Men working there were exempt from conscription to the armed services. The government took the extraordinary measure of inviting German industrialists to Coventry to see for themselves how advanced Britain was in its preparation for war. It was known that Germany was building up its military infrastructure. I suppose it was a calculated risk to demonstrate that Britain was more than ready for them.

Alongside the shadow factories was the vital manufacture of machine tools such as lathes. The industrialist Alfred Herbert set up the world's largest machine-tool factory, building a successful empire and great wealth which he shared with the people of Coventry. During nights of bombing, he watched the stricken sky over the city from his granddaughter's house in nearby Leamington Spa. She has told of how he would cry out for 'my poor men' and rush back to see the devastation the next day. His financial support for widows continued after his death in 1957, aged 90. We were proud of him as a great son of Coventry who worked through two world wars to produce munitions for Britain. His machine tools provided the horsepower for the city's heroic output by the shadow factories.

The Standard Motor Company had built its new production line on the golf course at Banner Lane, where it would make Bristol Hercules sleeve valve radial engines. Today a housing development is on the site. The Daimler works built its shadow factory in Browns Lane on some farmland where it turned out aero engines. There are houses there today, and an industrial estate. A second Standard shadow works was built on vacant land at Canley, making Bristol Beaufighter De Havilland Mosquitos. Houses stand there today.

H.M. Hobson made carburettors for aircraft engines on a new site in Canley and Humber acquired farmland at Ryton to build aircraft engines. Alvis built twenty sites in Coventry to produce military vehicles and munitions. Together these industries in my city built the air strength that would win our survival in the coming war.

Tens of thousands of local people were employed in war production and able to warn their families with authority that bombardments over our city were a certainty. Many people were so scared at the prospect that they refused to trust their safety to underground shelters and headed out of the city every night to sleep in their cars or on tarpaulin sheets in open fields – anything to escape the bombing. Others piled into the public shelters provided by Coventry city council and sat out the raids like that, eating sandwiches and playing cards, and keeping their spirits up with community singing.

There was a stoicism about the ordinary people around us. No wailing and crying, just getting on with it. The close neighbourhoods were, of course, a comfort. We knew everyone in our street and they knew us. People wanted to help each other.

Our school had a poor box where families would leave hand-me-down clothes and shoes, and the children on the receiving end wouldn't be belittled by others. Some children came from enormous families. I remember the Tweeds had twenty-three children! Mrs Tweed played the organ for the Salvation Army and her children were all well behaved and popular at school. My family was far from rich and we patched up everything to make it last. I learned to patch school knickers and darn socks – habits that are difficult to lose.

Years later my son-in-law looked at me in disbelief when I offered to darn his socks. It came from a lifelong habit of making do.

Clothes were rationed, along with many other essentials. We got twenty coupons a year for clothes and an overcoat took twelve, so it was important to make that coat last.

I never had a pair of gloves until a schoolfriend's kind mother took pity on me. I'd called for my friend Kath, an only child, at her house on the way to school one day, my hands blue with cold. Her mother, Mrs Gammon, brought me some navy-blue gloves she'd knitted. I treasured those gloves for years and would hide them in my coat pockets when I got home so no one else could have them.

I think the warmth they gave me was to do with Kath's mum's kindness as much as anything. She made cakes and buns and would always offer me one. In their house, with just Kath and her parents, it was always cosy and orderly, something I craved all my childhood.

At school I loved the discipline, which meant order and tidiness, a solid continuity to offset the chaos of life elsewhere. I valued the teachers. At secondary school I learnt domestic science, the essential art of cooking and budgeting for a family. We were each given a rag doll and taught to look after it as if it was a real baby. In those days, that was our perceived future. Girls would marry and have a family and stay at home. Factory work, which some women were employed in for the war effort, would end, and life would go back to its healthy normal. That was the mantra, that was the belief.

For now, I was enjoying the neat idea of a savings bank where I could store my pocket money. The government's National Savings Movement was enormously popular, a clever combination of appealing to the public to support 'our boys' fighting the enemy, and promising a good return for our money after the war. As children it was fun to hand over sixpence to buy a stamp, or half-a-crown to get several. Once you had the satisfying amount of £5-worth of stamps you got a Defence Bond. We would be able to cash it in for a lot more when the war ended.

And the incentive was irresistible: our money was funding the production of ships and weapons and aircraft. People of all classes, right down to small children like us, were lending their precious savings to the government. The theme was 'Save Your Way to Victory'. We felt as though we were personally contributing to the war effort.

The National Savings Movement was so successful there were 1,190 civil servants working full-time to run it by 1946.

Community groups in towns held a Spitfire Week or a Warship Week, and 'adopted' a warship or a fighter plane. In London, there was a big marquee with a captured German Messerschmitt fighter plane in it. You could pay one penny to go inside and get into the cockpit, working the control levers. The money went to National Savings. I was happy to put my pocket money towards this amazing national effort.

I loved geography and history lessons, where the wonderful Miss Lucas would enact scenes to help us remember important dates and events. She would physically act out the stealth of soldiers to reinforce our book learning, creeping round the classroom brandishing an imaginary sword or musket. I'll always be grateful for that grounding in life, the way our schools carried on educating us, despite the many disruptions.

Days without school were frequent, due to the bomb craters en-route, or a direct hit which had destroyed some classroom roofs. Sometimes we all huddled in the hall for lessons because other parts of the building had been bombed out. My sisters and I were in different classes at school because of our ages. I suppose I was a bit of a goody-goody because one day I saw my older sister Mary being led across the playground to my classroom by her teacher, to shame her by showing her my neat schoolbooks. Mary was always a bit rough and ready and careless. I felt totally humiliated by having to show her my books. She was grinning and sneering, refusing to feel ashamed. Close to tears, I told Mum as soon as I got home. Mary just laughed; she really didn't care. I never saw her cry; crying wasn't something we did at home. I kept a lot of my own feelings in, I'd learnt resilience. I wanted to be ladylike and have a different, ordered sort of life. At home there was shouting and chaos, and unhappiness between my parents. The war over Coventry, where we suffered forty-one German bombing raids between June 1940 and August 1942, put every family to the test. There was a bond, and the famous wartime spirit everyone remembers from the Second World War, but I still wanted to get away as soon as I could.

I would be leaving school at 14 and that would mean working for the war effort in one of Coventry's many factories if the conflict was still raging. I was ready for that. I wanted a life altogether more rewarding than the drudgery I watched my mum suffer. School was vitally important for me for as long as it lasted. I willingly walked the chilly, windy streets four times a day, to get there in the morning and return home for a midday meal in the years before school dinners were the norm. Then back to school and home again at 4 p.m.

One day there would be no going back after midday. I was walking home with friends, past the Dunlop Rubber factory and Courtaulds and the motor works which would later make Jaguar cars. We had nearly reached the park when we heard a German bomber, firing its machine gun. It swooped low over our heads in Holbrook Lane, firing mercilessly at men, women and children. Bullets ricocheted off the red-brick wall in front of Dunlop's. The men were on their way home for lunch – no work canteens in those days – and I saw them get off their bikes in a rush and come over to us to pick up the smallest boys and girls and get them to safety. We ran to the archway that leads to St Paul's graveyard and hid there, afraid and shocked. Children were crying but there was no screaming; we were speechless with fear. It was the first daylight raid over Coventry, a bold and ruthless action by a Heinkel bomber taking advantage of the low cloud cover.

Crouched in the archway I had a front-row view of the entire sortie. I saw the tell-tale black cross on the side of the aircraft and I saw the pilot himself, his leather helmet fastened under his chin, his goggles up on his head. I saw his bloated pink face and his bulging eyes. I felt this was a man who was making the war personal to us. He wasn't firing randomly; it was actually us he wanted to kill. Much later, I learned that his murderous action had already taken him down nearby Lythalls Lane where a young boy, his sister and a friend told of being in his direct line of fire as they took a pair of shoes to the cobbler's shop there. In later years the boy, Derek Beck, described how the cobbler pulled them inside and hid them under his wooden workbench as the bomber continued to strafe along the street.

He said when they emerged, the cobbler's windows had all been broken, the plane had come so close. 'As we were the only ones on the road it seems obvious the aircraft was deliberately gunning after children,' he told the BBC's *People's War* archive. His mother was so frightened that she called his father's works at the Alfred Herbert factory and left a message that she had taken the family to Tamworth. 'We left in such a hurry that Mum forgot to lock the front door,' Derek recalls.

After swooping down and firing at us in Holbrook Lane, the bomber went on to Canley, 5 miles away, to drop a huge load of bombs on the painting shop at the Standard

Motor works, firing on two sisters aged 16 and 11 as they crossed the highway. The older girl, Doreen Tucker, was an employee at the painting shop. She and her sister Kathleen told Coventry war historians that they ran across to an air-raid shelter, ducking the machine-gun bullets which were landing on the pavement all around them. 'When we got to the shelter, the ARP wardens were there to greet us and they said, "Oh my God, you're as white as snow,"' Doreen said.

It was 26 September 1940, a time when the London blitz was at its height. Our lone bomber must have veered away from the onslaught down there to make its own mark in the Midlands.

The capital city was suffering as never before. Bombing raids targeting family homes had started on 7 September and would continue for fifty-seven consecutive nights. The skies were black with 300 bombers overhead.

There were daytime air-raid warnings for two weeks in our city after that, though no attacks. It seems the Luftwaffe was concentrating its efforts on London. In mid-October, Coventry became its serious target once more, leading up to the most devastating attack of all, the one the world remembers. The one we call the Coventry Blitz, Hitler's furious reprisal for Britain's bombing of Munich and Berlin. The night we thought the world would end.

6

The Night Without End

The sirens started up their persistent wail at 7.10 p.m. and there was nothing unusual about that. But as we trudged out of the back door on the evening of Thursday, 14 November 1940 to head for the Anderson shelter, the rush of cold autumn air turned our breath to vapour. There was no need to pick our way carefully through the dark. It was as bright as day, with a full moon shining out of a clear sky. It seems that the government was well aware this would be no ordinary night of sporadic bombing. Less than a week earlier, the RAF had dropped bombs on Munich, the birthplace of the Nazi Party, on a night when Hitler himself was due to deliver a major speech.

This, coupled with Britain's refusal to sign a so-called 'peace offer' from Germany four months previously, encouraged Propaganda Minister Joseph Goebbels to promise his nation there would be 'total destruction' of Britain. He said the German public 'was burning to destroy Britain'.

Our government statisticians were predicting 4 million casualties in London alone, and coffins were being stockpiled.

Hitler personally issued the orders for the night-long carpet-bombing of the area at the heart of Britain's war production: Coventry, my city. There have been many years of deep controversy about whether Churchill and his government knew. The code-breakers working at Bletchley Park had deciphered signals that told of an onslaught on the night of 14 November, but, apparently, they could not be clear as to whether it would be London, Liverpool, Coventry or another major industrial centre. Churchill went up to the Air Ministry roof in Whitehall – as he did in advance of all bombing raids in the capital. Some historians believe he knew the target was Coventry but did not want to alert the Germans to the crucial information that we knew how to break their codes.

Whatever the information and how it might have been or should have been interpreted, it is clear now that there was little the government could have done even if Coventry had been correctly identified. The terrible truth, which no one was to know until that night, was that Germany was about to bring two major innovations into use. These were considered so successful in their destruction that they influenced all future strategic bombing raids for the rest of the war. They had developed the X-Gerät, the most sophisticated electronic navigation aid of its time, which would use multiple beams to direct bomber planes accurately towards their target for the first time. Transmitters were using a modulated radio signal on a higher frequency than the earlier Knickebein system, which the British were learning how to jam, and a fleet of German planes had been specially adapted to bring this new menace to our skies. The Germans were also about to unleash a hellish new mix of explosives and fire-bombs, literally setting the city alight at the same time as blowing it up. They had given the 14 November attack a special name – Operation *Mondscheinsonate* – meaning Moonlight Sonata, planned around the clear night and the full moon.

In our backyard, traipsing to the Anderson shelter, resigned to another night of noise and destruction and perhaps some fitful sleep, we soon realised this one was going to be different.

Even before the siren wailing had stopped, the first incendiary bombs were being dropped. It turned out that at 7.07 p.m., in Coventry's war room underneath the main post office, trackers had received the yellow coded message: 'Raiders approaching your area.' By 7.10 p.m. the message was coded red, meaning 'Air raid imminent' and the sirens sounded.

An initial wave of thirteen specially adapted Heinkel 111 aircraft, equipped with the X-Gerät devices, had crossed the British coastline at Lyme Bay in Dorset. They dropped 10,224 incendiary bombs and forty-eight high-explosive bombs. The result was eight huge fires. By 7.40 p.m., the roof timbers of our great medieval cathedral, St Michael's, had started to burn. Right behind that pathfinder fleet were 400 bombers stacked with the high explosives that would turn this into the Coventry Blitz, the most concentrated attack so far of the Second World War.

Fifteen minutes later, sixteen Heinkel bombers dropped eighty-four high-explosives and 2,412 incendiaries. After that, twenty bombers attacked the city every ten to fifteen minutes and this went on all night. Within the first half hour, almost all of Coventry's gas and electricity mains, water supply and telephone network had been destroyed.

The Provost of Coventry Cathedral, the Rev. Richard Howard, was on the roof with stonemason Jack Forbes and two younger fire-watchers when it was first hit. They saw the great north aisle in flames, and roof timbers were ablaze. Steel girders installed in an earlier restoration of the roof, and intended to strengthen it, were now red-hot and distorted, bringing the timbers crashing down with them. The Great West Door, made of solid Warwickshire oak, was reduced to ash. The provost and his team could do nothing but scramble to safety and watch from the south porch. The city's water mains had been destroyed; there was nothing they could do, even when an emergency team of firefighters arrived from Solihull. A bystander said afterwards he had been reduced to tears by seeing teams of courageous firemen carrying hoses unable to produce a drop of water against the growing sheet of flames.

We knew nothing of this tragedy as we sat it out in our shelter only a couple of miles away from the city centre. My dad saw the city alight, and people as far away as Nottingham and Wolverhampton have since talked of the fierce red glow all across the night sky as Coventry burned. My mum, sisters and I were huddled up in our siren suits and blankets trying to keep warm, frightened out of our minds by the incessant noise.

In the city centre, a westerly wind had whipped up the flames into one huge fire. Imperial War Museum documents show that one of the German bomber pilots, Flight Sergeant Handorf, described the destruction he helped to cause as 'a terrible beautiful picture of the most modern battle of destruction' as he flew home through cloud cover glowing a vivid red. The city was one huge 4–5-acre flame, with red-hot shrapnel raining down on houses, churches and factories.

The vicar of Holy Trinity – a church with one of the city's signature three spires – the Rev. G.W. Clitheroe, said he watched the destruction and compared it to an illustration for Dante's *Inferno*. He said, 'I wondered how we were going to be able to bury all the dead.'

By 8 p.m. there were 240 fires raging in Coventry. Brave firefighters paid the cost, with twenty-six dead and thirty-four seriously injured by the morning.

Our great fear, even as children, had always been that Coventry, at the centre of vital wartime production, would be a magnet for Hitler's bombers. The many factories turning out planes and engines, munitions and vital equipment, could be considered legitimate military targets. But our city, as the Germans certainly knew, had many residential areas around its industrial zones. Workers' housing had grown over the years, alongside the factories.

The Blitz was a cruel and sinister tactic intended to bring the suffering right into our homes. Britain had emerged victorious from the prolonged aerial fights during the Battle of Britain two months earlier. Our national pride in that had galvanised Hitler into a vicious war of revenge. That night in Coventry was his showcase.

My family and I had prayed our way through many a rough night of deafening noise. On 14 November that noise lasted literally all night. We could hear the anti-aircraft guns in the nearby stadium blasting away, and there were eleven other batteries all over the city. There were also sixty-four barrage balloons in the air, intended to keep German planes too high to bomb effectively. If they flew lower, the bombers risked entanglement in the hawsers keeping the balloons afloat. But we heard later that although our guns fired ten rounds a minute for the whole raid, only one German bomber was shot down.

The worst night of Britain's war so far – and one of the worst of my young life – lasted for eleven relentless hours. Statistics show that the raid reached its height at 11.45 p.m. and bombs were still raining down for hours after that. Thanks to their new navigation system, the Germans had time to fly back to their French coastal bases to re-fuel and re-arm, then return to drop more bombs. The longed-for signal, 'Raiders passed', reached the war room at 6.16 a.m., and the all-clear sounded at last.

In that one night of hell, 449 bombers reached Coventry, dropping 30,000 incendiary bombs, 64 flare bombs and around 1,600 high-explosive and oil bombs. More than 500 tons of bombs dropped on us that night. Official figures showed 568 people killed, 863 seriously injured, and 393 lightly injured.

Tens of thousands of people had driven out of the city in the early evening, in order to avoid further sleepless nights, and their absence and the huge number of transient workers made it impossible to assess how many had been killed or wounded. There are reports that some shelters were sealed and bodies never recovered. Many believe that the actual fatality numbers could be more than 1,000.

There was serious damage to 111 of Coventry's 180 factories; 624 shops were destroyed and the precious historic centre of the city – its medieval streets and grand half-timbered buildings – was all but obliterated. Three thousand people were made homeless when 4,330 houses were destroyed, and the immediate need was for food and shelter for a shell-shocked population wandering among the wreckage. Three-quarters of Coventry's buildings were registered as damaged and one-third of the factories seriously damaged. The trams and tramlines that kept our city moving had been badly hit in the bombing and, after that night, never ran again.

In the damp November morning, my sister and I trudged back to the house after the all-clear and got ready for school while my mother made our breakfast porridge. I suppose that was what they called the Blitz spirit: people just getting on with it no matter what Jerry was throwing at us. There was an air of fatality about Mum. It was one of those days when she said we would eat all our rations, 'because you never know if we'll still be here tomorrow'.

My father was exhausted after a night when his fire-watching duties had been totally impotent in the face of the onslaught. He had returned to the shelter to check on us several times, one time reporting grimly: 'The Browns' place has gone up in smoke. And all we've got if the fires come is a bucket of water and a stirrup pump.' During breakfast he said very little and all wireless and telephone connections were still down, so we had no clear idea of the aftermath of our endless night. But when we set off for school we got as far as the top of Masser Road and no further. Soldiers had screened off a massive crater and an unexploded bomb lay at its centre. These were a scourge throughout Britain during the Second World War. By the end, the army's bomb disposal units had defused 527 in Coventry alone. A further 167 blew up before they could be defused.

For us it would be a day off school. It wasn't until the following Monday morning that I stood in the school hall and listened to the head teacher read through a sad list of pupils we would never see again. She said there had been a direct hit on the Anderson shelter where one family was hiding and all except a school-age boy had perished. He had been dragged out of the rubble and was in hospital, unconscious and unaware he had lost everything – his entire family and home. We had seen rooftops caved in, broken windows and doors blasted out all around us, with rubble and glass strewn in the roads as we walked the familiar route from home to school.

It was a shock to see St Luke's Church. It had been the cornerstone of my young life. At 5 years old I was there for the funeral of my grandmother, burned to death in our home in front of my eyes. I was there every Sunday morning for Rev. Charles Dodd's service and returned after dinner for Sunday School. I had been confirmed there. Now the red-brick building was in ruins after a blasting during Blitz night and there would be no more comforting Sunday prayers and sermons for some time.

St Michael's Cathedral was a much grander relic. Soon after the entire edifice was reduced to rubble, the Provost

Richard Howard made a brave stand, instructing the cathedral's stonemason to carve the words 'Father Forgive' into a tablet of stone behind the remains of the high altar. He also fashioned a crude holy cross out of two charred roof timbers found in the debris, tying them together with some twisted metal. This was placed symbolically on the altar and is still preserved today on the staircase wall of the replacement cathedral.

Dick Howard, as all his congregation called him, is still today a legendary figure, a hero of Blitz night who saw the stark horror of it at close quarters but who also found it in himself to be quick to forgive.

His cousin, Rev. Michael Howard, followed in his footsteps as a member of the clergy at the cathedral and remembers him well. Today, Michael Howard is secretary of the Friends of Coventry Cathedral and recently wrote this tribute:

Provost Dick Howard, son of Charles Howard and Helen Bryan, was born in June 1884 in Cambridge where his father was Vicar of St. Philip's, near the railway station. He was actually my father's cousin and, being 25 years older than my father, he was more like a grandfather to me.

He was educated at Monkton Combe, a school near Bath which had been founded by his grandfather R.G. Bryan, and where his father had opened the Junior School, and where his mother had been educated.

Dick went up to Jesus College Cambridge in 1903 to read Maths as his father had done. He got a First and was a Wrangler exactly like his father (a Wrangler being a student gaining first-class honours in Mathematics). He then stayed for another two years to train for ordination at Ridley Hall and take a theology degree. He continued at his old college, Jesus, as chaplain.

He served as a CMS Missionary 1912–1918 to be Vice-Principal of St John's School (now College) Agra, near the Taj Mahal. Returning to Britain he was Principal of St. Aidan's Theological College, Birkenhead for ten years, and then became Vicar of St. Mary's Luton 1929–33. He was much involved with car factory workers there, so was happy to be invited to Coventry in 1933 to continue along the same lines, as Provost of St. Michael's Church, which had become the Cathedral for the newly formed Diocese for Coventry and Warwickshire in 1918. With war starting, the factories which had been making cars opened production lines for military vehicles and planes, and it was inevitable that Coventry would be a target for German bombing, so he had the stained glass taken down from the windows, as they were some of the very best in Britain, to be stored safely until the end of the war. Sure enough Coventry was a prime target for German air-raids. In September 1940, the Cathedral being very close to some of the old factories, a bomb fell on the Cathedral, perhaps accidentally, and its roof was damaged. They wondered whether if they painted KIRCHE on the roof in huge white lettering, the Germans would be more careful. Dick and the other Cathedral staff took turns on the roof each night as they anticipated further raids, and could perhaps smother the bombs in sand, and douse flames in water. Dick was up there on November 14th when the major onslaught took place, reducing his beloved Cathedral to smouldering ruins. His reaction: 'Father, Forgive'.

The Wyley Chapel became Britain's smallest cathedral until 1958 when, a few months after he retired, he carried the flame to the undercroft of the new cathedral, which it had been his last ten years as provost to lovingly shepherd into existence, with its ministry of reconciliation which he had begun in 1940 – as he outlined on BBC World Service on Christmas Day that year. He received many visitors from abroad, including from Germany.

Provost Howard had retrieved three large medieval nails from the rubble after his cathedral was bombed. He found them among the charred remains of the ancient rafters. He fashioned them into a rough cross and designated them a symbol of peace and reconciliation, making many copies and distributing them to churches, prisons and schools all over the world. His first trip abroad after the war was to Kiel in Germany, and the Cross of Nails he took there in 1947 for a service of reconciliation still hangs on the wall of their rebuilt church, the great church of St Nikolai in Kiel, the main city in Germany's Schleswig-Holstein.

Kiel had been carpet-bombed in the Second World War and the church destroyed. It was the first to receive a Cross of Nails. The provost returned to Coventry with a piece of St Nikolai's original masonry. The Cross of Nails gesture continues today.

The Rev. William Howard went to Kiel himself in 2017 for the seventieth anniversary of that first service of rec-onciliation. He describes a great affection for Coventry

Cathedral, having sung there for a Saturday and Sunday service annually with his school choir and having been shown around the building site of Coventry's modern cathedral by his cousin, the provost. He recalls that:

In retirement Dick Howard moved to Ufton Rectory as village Pastor until the age of 87, while he continued to write and teach throughout Britain and abroad. He kept a diary of daily thanksgiving to God and, more fully retired in Kenilworth, as he looked back over his long life he wrote a book listing thirty-three 'discoveries' of God that he had encountered through people, his reading of the Bible and in prayer.

Four years after Dick's parents' wedding his father's younger brother Alfred Howard had married his mother's younger sister Edith Bryan, so their children (including my father Stanley) were double cousins of Dick and his brothers and sisters. But Dick with his loving humour and deep faith was to me more like a grandfather. Now over forty years since he died aged 97, as I drive into Coventry, signposted as City of Peace and Reconciliation, I'm reminded of his amazing legacy.

As an 11-year-old girl in 1940, Provost Howard's generosity of spirit seemed at odds with the enormous suffering the Germans had caused. I knew that the words 'Father Forgive' came from the crucifixion of Christ himself, but I was confused about the notion of forgiving Germans and found Provost Howard's gesture hard to understand. I had a Christian upbringing and I believed in forgiveness, but the war was still continuing; the intense hatred of it was all around us. There was no sign of humanity in the Germans' activity, much less any contrition.

It was a long time before I could identify with the ordinary population of Germany who suffered at our hands during the RAF's bombing raids. We were all helpless, none of us wanting this war. I believe to this day that the men – nearly always men – who have our fate in their hands have no right to plan wars. Those intense round-table discussions they have should be directed at finding peace.

Today I have been heartbroken to see history repeating itself with the cruel bombardment of Ukraine by Russian antagonists. Television footage showing thousands of terrified, innocent people trying to shelter from bomb attacks brought it all back to me. I truly understood what they were going through. The world seems to have learnt nothing from the hell of Hitler's war. I always believed his own people did not realise the terror he was unleashing. But Putin's people know full well. How can they let this happen? I wept when I saw the crowds of frightened mothers and children, babies in prams with all their belongings, trying to flee the war in their own streets and homes. I know how scared they must have been. I've felt that fear myself. Britain needed help from the great powers of the world and America came to our aid. That is what Ukraine has needed since the start of the invasion. We cannot stand by and let war break Europe again.

My personal fight was to somehow get through it and emerge with a decent, happy life and I am certain that is how millions of Ukrainians are feeling now. Back then, I remember feeling that the adults in charge of our lives – from the powerful politicians to the heads of our own families – were making a bad job of it. Of course, there were heroes too. The ARP wardens and fire-watchers, the St John Ambulance Brigade, all the volunteers who worked as nurses and policemen during the day and tried to protect us at night, were our heroes. My schoolfriends and I saw them as our saviours. Along with our teachers they were the role models of our lives. They had rules, they could be strict disciplinarians, but through it all was caring and kindness. They were there to help and guide us, and to save lives.

In the aftermath of the Blitz in our city, they were working through the rubble and the broken glass, pulling out the survivors and the dead. It was terrible to hear of them alongside the soldiers, collecting body parts to put into sacks, ready for a mass burial.

Even public shelters had been hit, with devastating results. One Rescue Service worker, Albert Fearn, said he found two young women dressed up for a night out, one of them still holding her powder compact, dead in a shelter, their eyes open wide with shock. The Luftwaffe had proudly filmed its night-long activities and used the footage as propaganda. It announced a new word to commemorate its triumph: to 'coventrate'. The 'coventration' of a city was to blitz it to oblivion.

My schoolfriends and I heard that many people were travelling into the city centre to see the effect of the bombing for themselves. But my family didn't do that. We rarely went into the city; the bus fare was expensive and our lives were concentrated in the suburb of Holbrooks. There were shops on every corner, butchers and cobblers and grocery stores. We didn't need to go further afield and we felt no inclination to trudge around the debris in the remains of the cathedral or peer into ruined shops and homes.

There was an outbreak of looting but I believe it was soon dealt with by police and rescuers. Occasionally, the police would come by our house for a cup of tea and a chat with my dad about people trying to sell him stolen furniture from bomb sites. They gave him a list of missing items. Sometimes he was offered stolen jewellery. It is sad to think of people's most personal possessions being taken by fellow city-dwellers when the Germans were already trying to blight everything else in our lives.

We heard that King George VI visited Coventry two days after the Blitz. In full military uniform, accompanied by the mayor and the Provost Richard Howard, he had walked the ruined streets and greeted local people. He had stood in the rubble at the cathedral and been moved to tears. I supposed that to people who saw him it was a cheering, supportive sight. His visit had been unannounced, but even if we had known about it my family would not have rushed to the city centre to see him. Bracing ourselves for certain continuation of the bombing, we were exhausted and fearful. I remember we were not in any mood to cheer royalty.

An investigation by the government's Ministry of Information was already showing that Coventry people were extremely demoralised and worn down in the immediate aftermath of 14 November. The Ministry's Mass Observation Unit had sent representatives to the city the next morning and their findings backed up the general feeling of Coventry as a place extinguished.

It turned out that both Germany and Britain, unbeknown to one another, were anxious there could be a tipping point in public tolerance after mass onslaughts, and that this could lead to anarchy and disenchantment with the government of the day. This could spell defeat. Both countries desperately needed their people to put their hearts and souls into the war effort, to remain fiercely patriotic despite the turmoil.

In Coventry, the Mass Observation reporters looked for signs of mass panic. Their initial findings were alarming. A Ministry of Information report dated Saturday, 16 November reported signs of depression and hysteria. There was a widespread fear it might be all over for Coventry. People were inconsolable, some behaving wildly and irrationally. Matt Brosnan, a historian at the Imperial War Museum, said: 'The government was worried aerial bombardment could destroy civilian morale, and perhaps in Coventry those fears were put to their sternest test.'[1] The hysteria reached new heights when the local newspaper reported that people were still trapped beneath collapsed buildings, some of them still alive and being fed by tubes. Days later, the newspaper admitted this was untrue, but rumours persisted.

Churchill's cabinet was deeply worried. By nightfall on 16 November, families were driving out of the city in droves to find a place of safety in the surrounding countryside. They were certain there would be further nights of

1. BBC News piece published on 13 November 2015, the 75th anniversary of the Coventry Blitz, written by Jennifer Harby.

bombardment. Harrison reported that people were fighting to get places in strangers' vehicles and for those with no access to transport there was a deepening feeling that they had been abandoned. For my family there was a sort of torpor as we took to our shelter night after night, fully expecting further severe raids. Historians say that Germany might have consolidated its growing aerial superiority if it had continued to bombard Coventry.

That did not happen. We were spared further onslaught until many months later, although the air-raid sirens sounded regularly and the trudge to the Anderson shelter was frequently a feature of our winter evenings. Coventry people's demoralisation was partly because of our small size compared to London, Liverpool and Birmingham, and the closeness of our local communities, living cheek-by-jowl with the factories where the workforce were neighbours and friends. But it took just a few days for the city to find its true Blitz spirit. The government, worried that Coventry people were falling apart, sent 600 extra soldiers within three hours of the all-clear. Signals units restored the communications network, Royal Engineers blew up unsafe buildings and restored electricity, gas and water supplies. There were field kitchens and first-aid stations and 200 extra police on the streets to place a cordon around the vulnerable city centre. In the Council House – headquarters of the city council – a National Emergency Committee was set up. Stark handwritten notices went up on the walls outside to help people find their loved ones. It said: 'Enquiries re casualties, top floor. Enquiries re deaths, first floor.'

Rationing was suspended for seventeen days so that people without food or adequate clothing could buy whatever supplies were available. Hundreds of labourers and roofers were brought in to start tackling the huge task of rebuilding the city. Within five weeks, 12,000 homes had been repaired. Factories were partly operational again within two weeks, due to the need for workers to earn wages again and to a strong sense of defiance against the worst Hitler could do to us.

The government wanted to impose martial law but the city council leaders persuaded them otherwise. Coventry people would put things right themselves, and restore law and order, given time. A Ministry of Information van toured the streets with a loudspeaker, telling people where they could get hot food. An army of public-spirited volunteers swelled the numbers of Women's Voluntary Service, Salvation Army and Young Men's Christian Association members to bring the community back together in a united effort which impressed us all and began to breathe life back into the city.

There were about thirty relief stations handing out clothes and food, and seventeen mobile canteens toured the streets.

The Ministry of Health responded to a scare over possible waterborne diseases by inoculating around 100,000 people against typhoid. Someone climbed up the parapet of a ruined building in Broadgate and hung a Union Jack there. There was help and comfort for everyone. Coventry had rediscovered its heart.

But none of us dared to believe the bombing raids were over. People still poured out towards the countryside in vehicles, on bicycles and even on foot each night, not wanting to relive the nightmare of 14 November. Some people commuted into the city for work during the day and returned to the safety of the countryside at night. Many did this for the simple reason that their homes no longer existed; others were terrified of further bombing raids.

The weather was in our favour though. The damp, cloudy autumn days and nights, soon turning to winter, put paid to any further bombardments for a long time, and the Mass Observation Unit reported that the danger seemed to be over. Water supplies, although at a low pressure, had been restored within two days of the Blitz, and two days after that the postal system was back up and running. Within a fortnight, schools were functioning more or less normally and temporary shops had been built in Corporation Street.

Provost Richard Howard was holding church services in his own home now that he had lost his beloved cathedral, the only one in Britain to be destroyed in the Second World War.

The most tragic services of all were for the two mass burials of those who died on the night of the Blitz. The idea of mass graves was shocking, with its connotations of the workhouse and paupers' graves, but the city council used extreme tact to reconcile grieving families to the idea. They could all come together for a united service where vicars and chaplains and Catholic priests would read the funeral rites and where all could mourn together as coffins draped in Union Jacks would be lowered together into trenches. They called it a 'civic funeral'. Soldiers and gravediggers worked through the night to prepare the trenches at London Road cemetery. The 172 coffins were lowered, two deep, the mourners carrying wreaths and flowers, in a solemn ceremony befitting the overwhelmingly sad occasion.

A thousand people formed a quiet, respectful queue at the graveside. Throughout the funeral there were Spitfires and other fighter aircraft in the skies over the city, in case German bombers were heartless enough to make that occasion a target too. Three days later, a second mass burial took place at the same location.

The local authority funded these ceremonies, and was later reimbursed by central government. By the end of the Second World War, 808 local people had been buried at London Road cemetery. A total of 1,250 Coventry people were killed in the Second World War, some buried in other cemeteries in the city, some repatriated to their home towns in Ireland or Wales or elsewhere.

We had all lived in fear of further devastating attacks after 14 November but it was to be a fairly quiet winter; Germany had turned its attention to the big port cities and was also causing massive disruption to cargo fleets bringing food and munitions from America and Canada across the Atlantic. Then, in April 1941, out of the blue, we had a stark reminder of the Blitz night we had all been trying to put behind us. Once again Mum and I, with Pat and Irene, cowered in dread inside the Anderson shelter as high-explosive and incendiary bombs rained down for more than seven hours. There were direct hits on big factories like Courtaulds and Daimler and the Alvis Works and many dead in their homes nearby.

The bombers also mercilessly targeted the Coventry and Warwickshire hospital where many of the injured were being treated. It had ten direct hits which killed patients, nurses, doctors and stretcher-bearers. Worst of all, one bomb landed in the hospital entrance hall, causing a large crater, and medical staff put a wooden plank down to walk across it, not realising that hours after the all-clear it would explode, causing further deaths. The huge blast blew an ambulance from the street on to a top-floor balcony. The building collapsed, with nurses working to the last second to get patients to safety. Four nurses, including the matron, were awarded the George Medal for their bravery that night.

More than 280 people were killed. And two nights later the bombers came again, this time damaging Christ Church, the central post office, the Magistrates' Court and the Council House. Most of the dead were civilians. Once again it was the ordinary people of Coventry – people like us – who suffered the most. Once again there was no heating, power or water in the days to follow. The death toll from these two raids, ending on the morning of Easter Sunday, was 451, with 702 people seriously injured.

It meant more mass burials, but although the bombing was almost as severe as the night of the Blitz on 14 November, these were always referred to as 'the forgotten raids'. None of it was forgotten by us, the ordinary families just trying to get through it and survive.

My twelfth birthday was a few weeks later. I was growing into a determined, sometimes obstinate, girl with dreams of a life beyond the Blitz, beyond the chaos of my family home. It's impossible to say if those terrible bombing raids shaped my young mind; I certainly like to think there was no lasting psychological impact. But I know I was infuriated by the continual fearfulness and helplessness. I wanted to make a future for myself that was calm and orderly. I was always absolutely certain this was possible and that I would achieve it. You can pull yourself up and out of any situation, however bad, and achieve a good and decent life. I'd like to think today's young people can feel this and act on it without the devastation of war to drive them on.

While my city was still reeling from further German attacks, we had no way of knowing whether there would be another Blitz, but news was coming through that Hitler was moving troops en-masse to the east, near to the Russian border where he planned his next incursion. There would be six more raids over Coventry, causing ten deaths, the last one in August 1942. By then the government had begun to address the widespread problem of children's undernourishment. Thanks to the Welfare Food Scheme we all began to receive free cod liver oil, concentrated orange juice and vitamin pills. At school, there were individual bottles of milk at tuppence-ha'penny a week. Since I was made milk monitor, I was allowed a free bottle if there were absentees in the classroom.

At home, my mother was making hearty stews out of whatever scrag-end meat she could find at the butcher's, along with offal. I disliked eating heart or liver and she would cleverly disguise these in dishes like faggots or cottage pies. Anything to get us to eat and grow healthily. Our last night of misery in the Anderson shelter would be in mid-summer 1942 when we heard bombers coming over but there were no deaths.

Coventry's huge manufacturing base was back in business by then. Ours was a boom town again and even better, and exciting for us, the Americans had arrived. Among all the praise my city would receive in the aftermath of the Blitz – the resilience of the people, the twenty-four-hour working shifts in our great factories, the peace and forgiveness being preached in the ruins of our cathedral – the most significant is that our suffering helped to persuade America to join Britain in the war against Germany. Hitler had boasted to his people that they had annihilated Coventry on 14 November 1940 and in subsequent raids. Goebbels, his Propaganda Minister, announced that Coventry had been 'smashed completely' and that the munitions factories would never work again. But their triumphal tone backfired.

Well-respected newspapers in America, the *New York Times* and the *Herald Tribune* were reporting Germany's 'unfathomable barbarity' in deliberately destroying people's homes and their cathedral. It was partly due to America's horror at what happened to our city that it joined the war with us a little more than a year later and began to send its troops to Britain.

My sisters and I watched from our bedroom window as the Nissen huts went up in the greyhound stadium to house American soldiers.

There seemed to be hundreds of them in town. Four or five of them would be walking down our street and we'd go up to them to ask cheekily, 'Got any gum, chum?' and they would stop to chat. We'd only seen men like them in

American films; it seemed incredibly glamorous to have them here in Holbrooks. They were generous with sweets and chocolates, and nylon stockings for the older girls. And they held parties at their barracks with real bands. I looked forward to my fourteenth birthday when I could leave school and go out to work, have a job and some independence, and go to some of those parties.

Mabel (bottom right), aged about 7, with friends on a Sunday School outing before the outbreak of war.

Mabel, aged 17, in her office suit.

Mabel's parents, Jessie and Ben (far left and left).

Mabel's dad, Ben (right), and his brother, Phil, as young men.

Mabel's mum, Jessie, as a schoolgirl.

Mabel's dad, sleeves rolled up, 1956.

Mabel's beloved father-in-law, Horace, a hero of the First Battle of Ypres.

Clockwise from above:

John Hewitt, 16, in the early days of courting, 1945.

John, aged 18, in his Royal Navy uniform.

John on duty with HMS *Blackcap*, Stretton, February 1948.

Mabel out for a stroll with
John Hewitt in Coventry's
Memorial Park, 17 May 1948.

John and Mabel on holiday at Whitley Bay in 1947. From left to right: John, Mabel, Eileen (John's sister) and Horace (John's Dad).

Coventry Cathedral,
February 1949.

Wedding Day photos, taken at St Luke's Church.

Devoted dad, on holiday with Sandra (right) and Carole in Devon.

Mabel with the girls, on holiday in Devon.

A sunny day in the garden.

Mabel's family – the Swinging Sixties in the garden.

John and Mabel, still in love.

Mabel's childhood home in St Luke's Road, Holbrooks, as it looks today.

The archway entrance to St Paul's burial ground where Mabel sheltered from a German daylight raid.

Former Coventry Technical College where Mabel learnt her all-important secretarial skills.

Mabel and grandson Matt in her garden at the launch of Mabel's Enterprise.

Mabel enjoying her great-grandson Josh, aged 7 months, Christmas 2017.

Mabel, grandson Matt and great-granddaughter Beth, 2019.

Mabel, with her six siblings (from left: Pat, Irene, Rose, Mabel, Mary, Anne, Bill).

Mabel looking fabulous during her ninetieth birthday celebrations at The Ritz, London.

7

Finding John

They called it the 'friendly invasion' when half a million members of the American army and air forces came to Britain to link up with the RAF and help us end the misery of war. They seemed to bring Coventry back to life, holding children's parties and hosting dances with swing music we had never heard before. Even in the street they would hand out chewing gum, sweets and chocolates. They had a sort of swagger about them but they were polite too, always addressing adults as 'Sir' or 'Ma'am'.

It turns out they were under strict instructions to observe the English way of life. They had been told we were more reserved than them and wouldn't start conversations on trains or buses. They had all been issued leaflets giving them tips on how to treat us – and they were reminded that although they had come from a free country under no threat of war, we had been through a lot. They were no doubt shocked when they saw the devastating mess of Coventry's city centre. Their arrival brought some cheer and colour into our war-damaged lives. Certainly, local girls enjoyed an enriched social life.

My friends and I were too young to be invited to their parties. But we would hang around and be treated to sweets and chocolates.

I was by then very preoccupied with the idea of leaving school. Things had improved at home where my sister Anne had gone away to train as a nurse, my Uncle Phil had been courting and was now married, my oldest sister Mary was in service, and at last I had a bedroom to myself.

At school there were scholarship schemes which meant some girls could go on to further education and become lawyers or doctors. Places were limited to the top two or three in the school and, although I did well, I didn't make it to that level. I had loved my school years but work was going to be exciting too. Coventry was still buzzing with employment opportunities and girls of my age would go to the juvenile Labour Exchange in Lower Ford Street to see where we were needed in the war effort. All my friends were leaving school at the same time. Some of them enrolled with me for part-time courses at Coventry Technical College where we learnt shorthand and typing, the skills needed for any good job in administration. My dad paid the fees and I'll always be grateful to him for that.

The Tech was a local landmark in The Butts, a huge stone edifice with four sets of Doric columns, opened in a grand ceremony ten years earlier by the Duke of York, who had become King George VI by the time I enrolled there. The college later expanded and moved to another site, but the original building remains a pride of the city and has been preserved, although the interior has been converted to house the new Premier Inn. I spent happy times there, taking night courses on Tuesdays and Thursdays, and in one of Coventry's many periods of full employment there was no shortage of jobs for me to take up.

The Labour Exchange placed me at the Humber works, a major manufacturer of great motor saloons like the Humber Hawk and the Super Snipe. The factory spread across several acres, operating twenty-four hours a day in shifts. I cycled 4 miles there and 4 back, and I disliked it from the start. It was a vast place. When I look at the site today, developed as a huge housing estate, I can't believe I ever found my way around.

Humber had a grand reputation in the motor industry. When I joined at the most junior level, it was proudly turning out statesmanlike cars favoured by government ministers and royalty. Humber made the staff car for Field Marshal Montgomery, a Super Snipe with mineproof floors and long-range fuel tanks. It was his official transport in North Africa, Sicily and Italy.

When the car fell into the sea after the D-Day landings, Humber boasted that Montgomery valued it so highly he had it salvaged and back up and running within days. But for all Humber's wonderful reputation I did not enjoy being the lowest of the low – the junior who ran up and down the metal staircases and bridges across the factory floor, taking errands, sorting out the post and making tea.

The size of the place was overwhelming and impersonal. The main admin office was looked upon as some sort of holy corridor where employees like me were too lowly to even have access. I suppose I was learning something about the world of work but it didn't feel like it at the time.

I had skills that weren't being recognised or used. After six months I felt brave enough to tell the boss. Mr Lyons was an imposing presence in his big office with its glazed windows and doors, but he listened to me and agreed that I should go back to the Labour Exchange and try my luck in demanding a more challenging placement. My school records were examined and it was agreed that I was good at figures and deserved a chance at a better job.

I was given a place at the Co-operative Insurance Office, opposite the Council House, the headquarters of Coventry city council.

Mr Wilkie, a kindly man in a shiny waistcoat, put me in the clerical pool where insurance policies and payouts were recorded. Everything was done by hand: the adding-up of columns of figures and checking every ha'penny and farthing. There were no calculators in those days, no computerisation. Insurance agents went door-to-door collecting small sums from families on payday, timing their visits so they could be sure people would pay up before they set off for a night out. Many life insurance policies had been taken out in the 1800s and, despite many years passing, the payout would be just a small amount when someone died, although crucial in those years before welfare benefits. Each girl in my office was allocated a number of agents and we did their books. We were checking and double-checking, then taking the results to a senior clerk. There was no time-wasting, no clock-watching, and no talking during office hours.

At lunchtime we had sandwiches at our desks. Mum made them for me. My favourite was bread and dripping from the week's roast beef joint, or corned beef, ham or tomatoes. I was learning how to work in a team, how to reach daily targets and how to take responsibility. Those insurance claims, however small, were important to the lives of many thousands of people. It was valuable training that stood me in good stead for many years. And despite the continuation of war with Germany and the ever-present threat that carried, I managed to have a social life. I loved belonging to a group of close friends. Some of us were going to the night classes at Coventry Tech, and we'd all known each other from junior school to school-leaving age, or from St Luke's Church. Several of us were near neighbours. We hadn't had mixed classes at Hen Lane secondary school but there were boys in the same building and I knew some of them quite well.

I was very friendly with Gerald, a nice boy who went on to study industrial chemistry. We started a budding romance. But I was really sweet on someone else. John Hewitt was going out with one of my best friends and I knew she was also seeing someone else. So I waited for that situation to take its course, and found an opportunity to get close to him. John was a member of the local St John Ambulance Brigade where my sister was already signed up. My friends and I joined together as a little gang, meeting up weekly for first-aid training at the hall in our neighbourhood. We wore smart uniforms – grey dresses with a buckled belt and epaulettes. You had to pass an exam to join as a cadet, then we had practical lessons.

Everything was geared towards helping the victims of air raids, something we had seen for ourselves for years. We learnt how to treat breaks with splints, and how to apply triangular bandages. We practised chest compressions and handled stretchers. I did ambulance duties and passed more exams, eventually becoming a cadet officer.

John was already a sergeant. Like me he cycled to the Brigade's hall, and he began to wait for me outside when we were all leaving.

He was tall and slim with light-brown hair and a lovely smile. I was 15, coming up to 16, and I was already certain this was the boy for me, for my whole life. He was kind and well mannered, and quiet. There was no one like him in my noisy, chaotic family. One day he took my uniform beret from my head and cycled off with it, just for fun. The next day, a Saturday, I was in our living room with Mum and Dad, the tea table a mess of leftovers and dirty plates, the dog lying in front of the fire, and damp clothes hanging on a dryer overhead. Out of the window, to my horror, I saw John cycle up and make his way to the back door. I fled upstairs, dreading to think of his first sight of my home. I had been to his house where the St John Ambulance Brigade had occasionally held committee meetings. To me it was perfect, a warm orderly place with nice furniture and a welcoming feel. John's parents were polite and kind.

There was just John and his sister Eileen, so I suppose everything was calmer and there was more money to spend. John's father was good at DIY and had done a lot of work in the house. His mother was a milliner and there were signs of her sewing and design skills everywhere. It was a nice three-bedroomed house in Roland Avenue, Holbrooks, with a verandah outside, carpets on the floor and an electric cooker in the kitchen. There would be a tablecloth with china cups at teatime. Everything clean and neat. I loved all the comfort and care in John's home and the kindness of his parents towards me. I began to want this for myself.

Now he was seeing the way we lived at my home, the coal-house and the toilet in the yard and the scruffy dog and the washing. I felt I couldn't bear it. But I heard my dad opening the door to him and inviting him in. I was still upstairs but I was glad he wasn't being turned away at the door. I came down and found Mum had made him a cup of cocoa. He was chatting to Dad and if he was taken aback by his surroundings, he wasn't showing it. I walked up the yard with him to say goodbye and asked him fearfully what he thought. 'Your mum's lovely,' he said. 'And your dad's all right too.' John didn't care about my background or the way I lived. He cared about me.

It was to be a long-distance romance. He was an apprentice toolmaker at a local engineering works and although his call-up for National Service was deferred for six months – the government encouraged apprenticeships – we knew that he would be going away for two years once he reached the age of 18. It loomed over us, that terrible uncertainty of separation. Anything could happen in two years; either of us could meet someone else and forget this teenage relationship. We talked about it a lot. All our friends were going through the same thing, although for John and me there was a mutual determination to keep these feelings and stay loyal.

We would sometimes go to the pictures in town but that cost 1s 9d a seat and was a rare pleasure. We mostly went for walks, in the park or out to the countryside. In those days there were no coffee shops or disco dances, or social media, but the open Warwickshire countryside and farmland was on our doorstep.

We talked a lot, about our dreams of a future, about the war ending one day. We believed in Winston Churchill and his war cabinet. Tens of thousands of people in Coventry had thronged the streets when he came to see the aftermath of the Blitz and we had listened to his great speeches on the radio. By early 1945, his government was telling us the end was in sight, we were on the brink of victory over Germany. We wanted nothing more, John and I. Our city could be repaired and rebuilt, the rationing and austerity would end and we could have a life together in freedom.

He and his sister did not have such searing memories of the Blitz as I did. They had been successfully evacuated to Fenny Compton, a country village 26 miles away, and only remembered seeing Coventry burning on the skyline on 14 November. But now he had to do his duty and would be going away for two years. He had finished his apprenticeship and was now making gears for aircraft and cars. He had been selected to go into the Fleet Air Arm of the Royal Navy once he started his National Service. But we were to be lucky as he was never sent out to sea; he was mostly based at the military base at Bramcote, about 50 miles away. On weekend leave he was able to cycle over and I could cycle from my home to meet him in the middle somewhere. We believed the war was winding down. There was no more panic-stricken talk of Germany invading Britain. All the action was in Europe where hostilities were raging between Germany and the Soviets. So when we heard about the obliteration of Dresden – a large town with historic and cultural similarities to Coventry – it came as a terrible shock.

Just as our city's civilian population had been targeted and pulverised during the Blitz, now Britain and America had rained fire and explosives on to German people, and the death toll was a staggering 25,000 – more than four times the deaths we had suffered. The initial sense of revenge many Coventry people had felt in the aftermath of our Blitz had turned to sadness rather than anger over the previous four-and-a-half years. I believe nobody wished for any more death and destruction. But here were our leaders, claiming that Dresden had been a legitimate military target. And this followed the so-called 'area bombing' of Berlin, Hamburg, Munich, Cologne, Leipzig and Essen, all resulting in heavy civilian casualties.

It was the boasting in the national press which upset us; the claims that Coventry people would be happy about Dresden, about getting their revenge. John and I and our young friends were simply shocked to learn that ordinary people sheltering in their homes had been forced to suffer from relentless bombing just as we had. For them, the attacks had come without warning, so we also had that in common.

The RAF's Air Marshal Sir Arthur Harris – Bomber Harris, they called him – believed in bombing targets indiscriminately. Teaming up with the US Army Air Force, he had sent four massive raids over Dresden in a two-day onslaught that destroyed 6.5 square kilometres of the city.

Like Coventry, it had been a beautiful historic town with an important cathedral. Bomber Harris said it was a legitimate attack in that it hampered troop reinforcements coming from the west to defend Dresden from invading Soviet troops. The first wave of Lancaster heavy bombers and American B-17 Flying Fortresses destroyed railways, phone networks, gas, water and electricity mains. That was a direct echo of Germany's strategy in the Coventry Blitz. Dresden, Germany's seventh biggest city, was the country's largest unbombed built-up area. The first sirens had sounded there a few minutes before 10 p.m. and the first wave of bombing set the city alight. Further echoes of our Blitz. The big difference was that up to 200,000 refugees were trying to flee the city to escape the advancing Soviet forces and they took the brunt of the attacks, their burnt bodies stacked up in the streets. The next day the raids continued.

Back in Britain, the public was questioning our country's military tactics for the first time. It seems there had been a calculation of just how many civilians needed to be killed in order to completely destroy morale and have the city, and the country, clamouring for surrender. This was what Germany had planned for Coventry – to grind our people down until they deserted their jobs in the munitions industry and turned on the government, demanding a surrender. It hadn't worked in Coventry. Our people had come back fighting. And it didn't work in Dresden.

My lifelong conviction is that war is futile, planned by men in power with no regard or respect for the rest of us, the 'little people' who will bear the brunt of the suffering. Even Churchill tried to disown the annihilation in Dresden, but history shows that after a showdown with Bomber Harris he agreed that 'these attacks left the German people with a solid lesson in the disadvantages of war. It was a terrible lesson; conceivably that lesson, both in Germany and abroad, could be the most lasting single effect of the air war.'

The bombing of Dresden remains highly controversial. Coventry, our city, was proud to be the first community to decide on reconciliation, and a civic delegation led by the mayor made an official peace-offering visit to the East German city in the 1950s.

By 1956, Coventry had twinned with Dresden and a long tradition of mutual forgiveness and support began. It was hard for our young minds to comprehend the scale of aggression, followed by the pronouncement of peace. All we could really relate to was the suffering of those nights under attack, helpless with our families.

Soon there was an occasion for real, uncomplicated joy and relief – the announcement of the end of the Second World War and all its atrocities.

John was by now a member of the Air Training Corps, preparing for his National Service stint, and was away at camp when the celebrations began in earnest. Every street in Coventry – possibly every street in the land – had its own wonderful, rowdy street party.

St Luke's Road was alive with people bustling around, setting up trestle tables, bunting and Union Jacks every-where. People ransacked their own homes to find tablecloths and chairs, and we all made jellies and cakes, biscuits and buns, and sandwiches. Fish paste and meat paste sandwiches, a taste of wartime I don't think I'll ever forget.

Everyone had shared their butter and egg rations, and there were lights in every window for the first time for years. The street was lit up. Any men in uniform home on leave were our VIPs; they deserved the loudest cheers of the day. It was a party to end all parties. One of our neighbours had a record player and loudspeakers. We sang all the war-time favourites – 'Roll Out the Barrel', 'Knees Up Mother Brown' – and all the troops' bawdy favourites. We drank home-made beer and wine, and we did the Hokey-Cokey. I was just 16, and I was happy to dance in the street with neighbours and friends out of joy and relief.

By now I had decided to leave the Co-op Insurance Company and work full-time for my father. He was exhausted after years of juggling his business concerns – the lorries he now owned for furniture removals, the little greengrocery, florist and grocery shops he had in the city centre and the terraced houses he had bought as a hedge against hard times. All of his earnings had gone towards the family or the business. There was no wealth in property in those days, and his small-time enterprises could not compete with new, smarter shops springing up with young, ambitious owners. Dad's health was suffering too. A Woodbine smoker all his adult life, he had a hacking cough and weak chest. The winter-time bouts of bronchitis became a regular problem, and at that time there were no antibiotics available for chest infections. He needed my help, and my status inside the family was increasing as I proved myself at a steady job which was giving me accounting and book-keeping skills.

My friendship with John had brought about a difference too. He had a good relationship with my father, treating him with respect and bringing his own experience of the world of work into many a long chat around the fireside.

They talked about the changes we could expect from post-war Coventry as its wartime damage was repaired, and there were big plans for a modern city centre. Coventry city council had brought in a new dynamic architect and town planner, 29-year-old Donald Gibson, who had a grand vision for our commercial future. He saw our war ruins as a chance to build anew. His plan involved a huge pedestrian shopping precinct to replace Broadgate, the central street most heavily bombed in the Blitz. Medieval buildings and slum dwellings would be cleared and new, low-level buildings would complement the cathedral and Holy Trinity Church, the pride of our city. Some ancient buildings would be preserved as important reminders of Coventry's proud history – the place where English kings had once lived. In 1948, Princess Elizabeth, our future Queen, came to lay the foundation stone for a brand-new shopping precinct.

At home I was looking at many years' worth of our household accounts. Small businesses like my father's were going to the wall. I realised that all the money he earned in his various jobs – the removals, the house-clearances, the coal hauling – had been spoken for. And younger men were starting up with the help of government grants for the regeneration of our city. He needed me to help his finances stay afloat. He was selling some of the terraced houses and other properties but he intended to keep the businesses viable as long as possible.

I set up office in our front room, the same place where he had laid out all his bank notes to dry after a bomb had blasted him into the brook. Some days I cycled into town to do a stint serving in the shops. I didn't enjoy it; my skills were better suited to the nuts and bolts of the business, the invoices and accounts and tax records.

But there was a nostalgia about the area which pleased me a lot. John's father Horace, a kindly man who had welcomed me into the family from the start, had told us a romantic story about how he met his wife, John's mother. He had returned from the First World War in a very bad way, thin and emaciated from years in a prisoner-of-war camp. He had fought with the Royal Warwickshire Regiment on the Western Front in Belgium and remembered the unofficial truces in Christmas week 1914. He and his fellow soldiers, exhausted from the First Battle of Ypres, had sung Christmas carols in their trenches and heard the Germans nearby singing their seasonal songs. The trenches were so close to one another, the British and Germans could shout to each other. They talked about football and the weather, and their families back home. Horace remembered climbing out of his trench and meeting German soldiers in No Man's Land, exchanging cigarettes and food. A football was kicked around and the strange camaraderie led to joint burial services and an exchange of prisoners. Both Germany and Britain disapproved strongly and wanted their men to get back on a war footing.

In a later battle, Horace was taken prisoner. He told us the food rations were at starvation level and the food itself was all but inedible. He remembered dry, black bread and stews made from unrecognisable ingredients. He had nearly starved to death. A piece of shrapnel was lodged in his thigh and stayed there for the rest of his life. Later, when his grandchildren climbed on to his lap, he would move it to get more comfortable.

He told us how one day he had watched while a horse and cart brought a cargo of cider to the prison camp for the German staff. There were large wooden barrels, and Horace saw that, as empty barrels were being loaded for the return journey, one had fallen from the cart and its lid had rolled off. He climbed inside, pulling the lid on, and found himself loaded on to the cart and bumped and jolted over a rough road for many miles.

He stayed in the barrel, struggling to stay upright, until it reached its base. At nightfall he crawled out and ran into the countryside, sheltering in a barn. The farmer's wife discovered him in the morning. Fortunately for him, she was sympathetic and found him some farm labourer's clothes and contacted members of the local Resistance movement. They drew him a map, and wished him luck in getting to the coast. The farmer's wife took his address in Coventry and sent a letter to his parents. On it was just one sentence in French. The family had to ask Coventry city council to help them translate it. It said: 'Your son is alive, on his way home.' Today that postcard is one of our family's most treasured possessions. Horace made it to Dieppe and back to his parents.

Another cherished memento is a letter from King George V, welcoming him home. Dated simply 1918, on Buckingham Palace headed notepaper, it is handwritten and reads:

The Queen joins me in welcoming you on your release from the miseries and hardships which you have endured with such patience and courage … We are thankful that the longed-for day has arrived and that back in the old country you will be able once more to enjoy the happiness of home and to see good days among those who anxiously look for your return.

It was signed George R.

It took a long time for Horace to regain strength. For many months, his parents tried to feed him gently back to health. They lived in a tenement building above a row of shops in Hertford Street – close to Spon Street – overlooking an inner courtyard shared by several others. During his recovery, his parents would help him out to the courtyard to sit in the sunshine. Millie, a pretty girl learning to make hats at a milliner's workshop across the yard, looked across at him. Her boss, a kind woman, gave her some soup to take over to him.

And that was how their romance grew. Horace gradually recovered his health and strength and they got married, still very happy together when I came into their son's life.

John was proud of his parents and their background. I had never seen that closeness before and it was what I wanted for my own future family. John and my father got on so well, chatting about business, money and world affairs. It gave me a new status in my family; I was beginning to be treated like a grown-up. When we talked about getting married and having a family of our own, I was adamant – John would not treat our children the way I had had to live. He would not dominate their lives and rule by fear. We agreed there would be no serious rows in our home. My childhood had been blighted by the sound of my father shouting and ranting at my poor mother. I was absolutely definite that we had to do things differently. I knew I could be obstinate, and even sulky when I didn't get my way. I gave John the silent treatment only once, and he put it to me, 'We're going to be married for a very long time. You can't sulk your way through all our years together. We need to talk things through and clear up problems before they go any further. The sulking has to stop.' I believe that was the foundation of our relationship, talking things over and respecting one another.

We had five years in which to build our feelings for each other. It was all about love and hope, a new beginning after so much war in both of our lives. His call-up for National Service had been a testing time but we got through it and I never seriously looked at another boy.

My whole social life was centred on the St John Ambulance Brigade where I had a good network of friends and fellow volunteers. We had training sessions and committee meetings, and also Saturday night parties and dances. There would be a live four- or five-piece band with a glamorous singer, and we waltzed and foxtrotted around the dance floor. My mother made me full-length dresses with swirly skirts and fitted bodices, and neat little cuffs on the three-quarter sleeves. All the girls dressed to the nines and the boys wore suits. My favourite was the tango, with proper Argentinian-style music. And we learnt the jitterbug, an exciting new craze brought in by the Americans. It wasn't *Strictly Come Dancing* but it was our wonderful Saturday nights out. I can't say there weren't romantic temptations, and quite a few offers, but John remained the love of my life.

One Christmas Eve, when he was home on leave from the Fleet Air Arm, he came to my house in a serious mood. My parents had gone to the nearby pub for their usual Saturday night drinks and we had the place to ourselves. I made some tea and was bringing it to him by the fire when he stopped me in the doorway. He took me in his arms and asked me to marry him. We both knew for certain that I was going to say yes. He slipped an engagement ring on my finger and we felt like the happiest, most blessed couple in the world. Standing there in that dingy little kitchen with no material wealth to our names, not a drop of champagne in sight and a life of hard work ahead of us, we were happy beyond belief. We had love and hope and that's all that mattered.

My parents didn't even pretend to be surprised. They had known all about the proposal and the ring. What mattered now was to save up enough rations for a feast on our wedding day. We set the date for 22 July 1950.

8

Beyond the Blitz

We had planned a summer wedding, hoping for July sunshine. Instead, there was nothing but grey skies and persistent rain all day and well into our honeymoon. But nothing could dampen the excitement as my sisters and friends bustled around the house to help me get ready. My brother, Bill, was away in the army but all five of my sisters were there.

The local corner shop had helped us to plan a feast: a three-tier wedding cake and a cold buffet of ham and corned beef salads, and jellies. My dress was borrowed from my friend Kath. Clothing was still rationed in 1950 and it would have been impossible to find enough coupons for a dress of my own. Kath had married a few months earlier and bought some lovely white fabric to make her own dress.

We were the same height and build so it fitted me perfectly. I bought a pretty headdress and borrowed a veil. I loved the glamour and fuss of it all, fixing my hair and lipstick and coming downstairs to hear all the family's approval before setting off for St Luke's Church.

I had three bridesmaids: my sister Rose, John's sister Eileen and my best friend Jessie.

Finally, there was just Dad and me in the house, waiting for the taxi. He was smart in a suit and looking, unusually, a little emotional. As we drove towards the church, I'll never forget him telling me, 'I want you to be sure about all this. If you want to change your mind there won't be any fuss, I can tell everybody for you.' Changing my mind was the last thing in the world that I wanted to do. But I realised that Dad was mellowing; he was no longer the cold, strict parent of my childhood. As I walked up the aisle on his arm, there was John in his best suit and tie with a buttonhole. My family were such loyal churchgoers that the vicar said we could go up to the altar itself for the ceremony. There were hymns and prayers and a wonderful feeling that life would be good from now on. We had such modest plans – a hard-working life, saving for a home of our own, a little family and really just being together in love. That was enough for me.

As we left the church to walk to the nearby hall for the wedding breakfast there was an archway of splints from our friends and colleagues in the St John Ambulance Brigade, all smartly turned out in their uniforms, the perfect send-off. We had a slightly mad idea that it would be romantic to head for our honeymoon in North Wales on John's motorbike. Despite the rain we kept to our plan. It was more than 150 miles to Llandudno and no motorways had yet been built. My 'going-away outfit' was bike leathers and a helmet. The romance of the day began to wear a bit thin as we headed into the driving rain and at one point we skidded round a corner where there was gravel in the road and we both came off. Amazingly the bike was okay and we travelled on.

Our hotel was on the seafront and arriving at midnight we were grubby and soaking wet, surprising the night porter who was expecting a pair of glamorous newlyweds. Sympathetic, he made us a hot drink and took us to a lovely room with sea views. Exhausted, we fell into bed and had an uneventful wedding night.

We spent a week touring the countryside on John's bike, happy in each other's company and making plans for our first home. My dad had already told us that he was buying another little house and we could live in it rent-free, saving as much as we could towards a home of our own.

I realised that since John had come into our lives my father seemed to appreciate me and the skills I could bring to his business, and actually wanted to be supportive. It was touching that he wanted to help us set up home. John had broken the ice in a way none of my sisters' husbands had, and Dad had become someone we could talk to. He respected the fact we had a savings plan, especially as my sisters were not good with money, frittering everything on clothes and not giving a thought to the future. My brother, Bill, would soon be leaving the army and had notions of helping Dad run his business. I was worried that he wouldn't look after the books properly. But now I was married and that meant I had a full-time job running a home and starting a family and Bill would be taking over. I was anxious that the smooth-running office I had set up at my parents' house might go downhill.

Dad offered us a flat over a shop he owned in Foleshill to live in while he arranged the purchase of a terraced house in Abercorn Road. He was planning to live there himself with my mother once they had retired. That gave us some time to collect together second-hand furniture. Anything new was out of the question. Timber was in short supply because much of it came from abroad, and there was huge demand for the rebuilding of homes damaged in the war. The only furniture you could buy came under the government's Utility Furniture Scheme started in 1942. It was sturdy but basic. John and I chose some items from Dad's second-hand furniture business instead. By the time we moved into Abercorn Road I was pregnant with our daughter Sandra. Everything was moving on in our lives, and in our city.

I had seen for myself the destruction caused by bombing in the centre of Coventry. Cycling to and from work at the Co-op insurance office and walking around the town with my friends, it was obvious to us that the old heart of the place had gone forever. In fact, the city planners, especially the ambitious Chief Architect Donald Gibson, already had grand plans to completely modernise the place and make it some sort of showcase. Hard to believe that Coventry was once, many centuries ago, the best-preserved medieval market town in Europe. Now, having listened to the city council's proud announcements and seen the scale models it produced for 'The Future Coventry' exhibition in Queen Victoria Road's Drill Hall, we feared it was going to become some sort of concrete monstrosity.

That's how my friends and I saw it. We read of the public outcry against the new minimalist plans, the sweeping away of traditional old buildings to make way for a pedestrian shopping precinct on two levels.

Most outrage was directed at the rebuilding of the cathedral. We had all spent time in the rubble of the bombed ruins, taking a path the firemen had cleared all the way to the altar. The days of marvelling at the sun shining through stained-glass windows were gone. Instead, the only thing that shone, now picked out in gold, were the words 'Father Forgive', inscribed behind the altar just days after the Blitz. The futility of what the Germans had done, smashing our history, still made us angry despite Provost Richard Howard's altruistic attempts at reconciliation. Now we were having to clean up the mess and would never see the likes of our grand gothic cathedral again.

The controversy over its rebuilding had been raging since 1944 when the first architect asked to propose a design, Sir Giles Gilbert Scott, had his ideas turned down as too traditionalist, too old-fashioned. He resigned in protest and a nationwide competition was announced, bringing in more than 200 entries. The modernist architect Basil Spence was chosen to create the new cathedral. His master stroke seemed to be the retention of the ruins, which were stark and beautiful in themselves, open to the skies, alongside a new contrasting structure. Just yards away from the ruins, where beautiful sculptures would be placed in memorial to the dead, the new building had its foundation stone laid by the Queen in 1956. Six years later she returned for its consecration, with Benjamin Britten's *War Requiem*, composed for the occasion, played and sung for the first time.

The building was highly controversial, with local people complaining it was 'a horror' and looked like a super-cinema. I have never come to love it, that huge impersonal open space and lack of intimate atmosphere that I've always associated with holy places. But times change. In 1999, the new cathedral was voted Britain's Best-Loved Building of the past 100 years, in a national poll by English Heritage. Certainly, Coventry has come to be proud of it and there is no doubt it serves as a symbol of peace and reconciliation, thanks mainly to the provost. He had been quick to see the importance of achieving forgiveness between Coventry and similar-sized cities which had suffered as badly. As early as Christmas 1940, just weeks after our night of the Blitz, the provost had broadcast a service from the ruins and said, 'We're trying, hard as it may be, to banish all thoughts of revenge … We're going to try to make a kinder, simpler, a more Christ-childlike sort of world.'

Provost Howard was instrumental in bringing about an extraordinary bond of peace between Coventry and other cities which had suffered. The war had not yet finished when we twinned with Stalingrad, the Russian industrial city where 40,000 civilians died in German bombing raids and there were more than a million Soviet forces' casualties. The working people of Coventry had sent their own gestures of support and sympathy to Stalingrad, and it became the first official twinning in Britain in 1944. In 1947, we twinned with the East German town of Kiel, and in 1956 with Dresden itself, like us a potent symbol of the evil of carpet-bombing. Today Coventry has links with twenty-six foreign cities through the twinning system, including the war-torn cities of Sarajevo, Warsaw and Arnhem.

I've always thought of Coventry as a city with a good heart. It's smaller than many other British cities, with communities who have remained close. Once a walled town with a castle, a cathedral priory and a bishop, it was on several occasions the capital of England. King Henry IV held Parliament here in 1404 and Coventry was sufficiently wealthy to fund Henry V and VI to fight wars with France.

The wool trade had brought it great wealth, with the River Sherbourne providing water power for the mills, timber readily available from the Forest of Arden, red sandstone quarries nearby for building materials, and the great arable lands supporting sheep that provided the wool. The Roman roads of Watling Street and the Fosse Way were the trade routes.

When the wool and dyeing industries declined, silk and ribbon weaving brought about another boom, boosted by the opening of canal links and a railway line. In 1861, as the economy was once again threatened, enterprising investors from London set up the Coventry Sewing Machine Company to produce sewing machines and later bicycles. The city became a byword for transport innovation. Highly skilled workers in the watch- and clock-making trade adapted their talents towards early car manufacture.

Britain's first car was made in Coventry in 1897 and a quarter of the entire population worked in the cycle and motor trade. There was trade boom after trade boom. Courtaulds textile works brought the silk industry into the twentieth century, producing nylon, the first man-made fibre.

The outbreak of the First World War brought further wealth. Guns, munitions, vehicles and aero engines were the mainstay of Coventry's employment. There were 60,000 people working in war production here by 1918. Coventry's importance as the heart of Britain's crucial munitions and machine-tool industry increased as the near-certainty of another major war with Germany loomed. By mid-1940, the population was growing by one thousand a month. The Ministry of Information's Mass Observation Unit carried out a survey for the National Savings Movement and found prosperity in the city streets. Long working hours and high wages meant that average incomes in Coventry were higher than in London. We were a boom town again and that clearly worked against us once Germany had identified us a desirable target.

But even the intensity of their bombardments hardly slowed production, and the engineering skills acquired by tens of thousands of workers later proved to be easily adapted to the manufacture of motor cars. By the end of the Second World War there was renewed demand. The Coventry of my early married years was enjoying yet another surge of wealth. People had money in their pockets. They worked hard, often doing twelve-hour shifts, and they wanted to enjoy their leisure time. The rebuilding of the city centre gave them bowling alleys, cinemas, hundreds of shopping outlets in the new pedestrian precinct, and the Locarno ballroom.

Later generations, including my own two daughters, would enjoy all this. But back in the early 1950s, aged 21, all I wanted was a comfortable home, financial security and a peaceful, happy marriage. I was conscious of my city's journey over the centuries from quaint medieval market town to booming industrial centre, with war-ravaged years in between. But my personal world was small. I was still trying to put a chaotic childhood behind me. John and I had each lived through a lot of war. Now we were bringing our first child, a daughter, Sandra, into the world.

It hadn't been an easy pregnancy and for the first few weeks I had trouble feeding the baby. She wasn't digesting food properly and she wasn't putting on weight. She wasn't thriving and was sick after every feed. I had to have a bucket nearby to catch the projectile vomit. By chance we had a midwife as a close neighbour. She was so alarmed when she saw baby Sandra in her pram one day, looking pale and weak, that she insisted I went straight to the welfare clinic. I was called to the front of the busy queue and a kindly doctor gave me a letter for the hospital, telling me I should go there urgently for a diagnosis. The hospital was nearby and a consultant there wasted no time. He examined my baby, then picked up my hand. He said, 'Now mother, come here and feel this little lump. I need to take that away and I need to do it soon.'

Sandra had pyloric stenosis, a rare condition which blocks food from leaving the stomach and entering the duodenum, part of the small intestine. It was a medical emergency which could have ended her life.

I had to leave my baby at the hospital and hurry home to tell John. There were no facilities for mother and baby to be together in those days. In six weeks of hospitalisation, I could only see Sandra at visiting hours, taking a fresh supply of terry-towelling nappies for her use as the hospital did not supply them, and disposable nappies had not yet been invented. I will never forget the first time I saw her after her operation. Her little arms were tied to the sides of the cot, so were her legs, and there was a huge cotton pad on her tummy. She was fast asleep, sedated, with eleven stitches down her tiny front.

Everyone in the street knew about those anxious six weeks. Neighbours brought home-made cakes and pies to the door, and if there were nappies on the washing line when it rained and I was out, they would bring them in. The close community we lived in, the neighbourliness that had led the midwife to look in Sandra's pram and identify a problem, had literally saved her life.

But John and I longed for a home of our own. I was a full-time mother and housewife and John was doing well as a toolmaker at Nuffield Tool and Gauge which was part of Morris Motors.

We had ambitions but they weren't at all fancy. We'd been through a lot so we knew how to value the small things – a happy home and family life. We had saved well and were ready to buy our own little house, just as my father's health was worsening and he wanted to retire. My brother, Bill, had, as I'd anticipated, run the business pretty well into the ground. My parents needed to sell up their remaining assets, to stop struggling and have a quieter life. John and I managed to get a mortgage and found a terraced house in Rookery Lane, so my parents were able to move into Abercorn Road.

By the time little Sandra was ready to come home from hospital we had moved in. The next-door neighbours, watchful as ever, suddenly noticed a baby in residence. They actually asked me if we'd adopted her. Sometimes the close community was just a bit too interested in their neighbours' lives. Rookery Lane was part of the mining area in those days. There were women who went knocking door-to-door to sell bunches of lucky heather and if you didn't give them money, they would mutter a 'tinker's curse' at you. It was frightening for children and I remember hiding under a table once with Sandra to avoid answering the door, only to emerge a few minutes later and find the woman peering into the window straight at us.

Our next-door neighbour kept pigeons in a shed in the garden and these were a terrible nuisance when I had washing on the line. The husband was a big drinker and we heard a great deal of swearing and shouting on a Sunday when he had come home from the pub and his dinner wasn't on the table. There were rats in the nearby fields and we could hear them in the roof space, running along from house to house. Children from the family who lived opposite would sometimes run into the road to use the gutter as a toilet. My daughter Sandra says today that her earliest memory is the stained glass in the front door of our house. It was a common feature of pre-war terraced houses, a bright-red galleon in full sail across a clear blue sea, with white clouds in the sky. I'm glad she remembers something positive about it but this wasn't the life I wanted to lead. These conditions had plagued my childhood and I was more determined than ever to put them behind me and find a better way to live.

Baby Carole came along three years after Sandra, and I had my hands full. But we had made a mistake with the house. At that time the area was worryingly rough, and we discovered it was prone to subsidence, built as it was over the old Keresley coal-pit.

I was on my way out to go shopping one day when I closed the front door and heard a strange noise. I went on my way, then came back to put the baby down for a nap and found I couldn't open the bedroom door. The ceiling had completely fallen in, not a piece of plaster left on it. There was choking plaster dust everywhere, and we came to realise that the floorboards were not level, there were cracks in the walls and gaps between the floorboards and the skirting. I remember it cost £11 to patch up the ceiling, at a time when £12 was a week's wage.

That whole side of the town was suffering subsidence. We needed to find somewhere new and safe to live. By this time we had some savings. A local solicitor advised us against making the same mistake again, telling us to look for a house on the other side of Coventry, an area we felt might be too expensive. Many new housing estates were being built in the suburbs to accommodate the thousands of people made homeless by the war and the many incomers who were snapping up jobs in the thriving motor industry.

We were lucky to find a new three-bedroom house with light airy rooms and big windows, and a muddy plot that could be turned into a family garden. We managed to scrape up the deposit for it.

It was in the suburb of Styvechale and was to become my forever home, the place where I still live. We were delighted with it even when it was still empty and the garden plot was bare. We used to go there to fix curtains and plan where to put furniture, and John would straight-away light a fire in the grate to cheer the place up. I cooked pikelets with a toasting fork over the flames and we all sat in the unfurnished sitting room, enjoying the novelty of a new beginning.

John's skills in helping the young apprentices at the Morris motor works were being noticed and he was told he would make a good lecturer if he gained teaching qualifications. He decided to work night shifts from 10 p.m. to 6 a.m. so he could study in the afternoons. He would be there to see the girls off to school after I had left for work, then get some much-needed sleep before swotting for his exams. It took four years of hard work to attain his degree in education at Wolverhampton University, then Morris promoted him to a position as full-time lecturer for their trainee schemes at Henley College of Further Education. He ran a pilot course which was so successful that more lecturers were taken on and apprentices began to be sent there from the Rolls-Royce works and other major car and engineering factories in Coventry.

He had a really soft spot for the lads who were struggling, always making extra time for them. He told me one day about a teenage boy who arrived early at the college workshop, looking scruffy and unwashed. He had had a row at home the previous evening and his father had thrown him out. The poor boy had slept rough. John, typical of him, took him to the college canteen and gave him breakfast. He told the canteen staff about the boy's plight and a kind-hearted woman there took him in and made him a permanent part of her family. Years later he came knocking at our door one evening, wanting to thank John. He had come through the difficult times and now had a good career and a settled life.

One of the proudest moments of my life was when the college produced a special annual award in John's name, an engraved trophy for the apprentice who had tried the hardest that year, a perfect tribute to the way John cared for the underdog. John would have been very unhappy in recent years to see the demise of apprenticeship schemes like his. They were the bedrock of the city's great industries and gave young people a solid start to their working lives. I'm glad to see apprenticeships being brought back.

Our family was thriving by now, happy with our new home and the garden where John planted shrubs and an apple tree, all still flourishing today. The girls were settled at school and our extended family was all around Coventry, my sisters and my brother all married with children. They could sometimes be a little bit catty about what they perceived as my elevated status, living in a good neighbourhood with a lovely home. But I had been adamant since childhood that I wanted a better life than the struggle and drudgery my mother endured.

It wasn't my fault that several of my sisters now lived in poor areas with little money. My favourite sister, Anne, and I had stayed close through the years but now she was living in the Woodend council estate, which was pretty rough. When we drove over to see her, John would insist on parking the car directly in front of the window so he could see it. There was every chance the local kids would damage it, steal the tyres and leave it standing on bricks at the roadside. I once drove over there alone and found the car doors vandalised when I left; a senseless attack from locals jealous of a possession they couldn't afford.

On most Sunday afternoons we went for tea at John's parents. There were home-made cakes and we all sat together at the table.

That was really important for my family; John and I always insisted on taking meals at the table with the children. There were no TV dinners, or sandwiches on a plate while everyone was glued to the box. We had conversations about everything at the dining table throughout the girls' childhood and they tell me now that they appreciate it. Manners were important and it makes me proud to see these important rules instilled in my grandchildren today.

Sandra and Carole were happy, well-rounded children. We didn't have rows in our house, ever, although things could occasionally get lively.

When I was keen to learn how to drive, I had some paid lessons then John said he'd take me out. We got as far as the next couple of streets from our house when he teased me about my lack of skill and I stopped the car to storm off home without him. On the way back in tears of anger I saw him sail past me in the car. Our next-door neighbour asked me what was wrong, and confessed he was having the same problems teaching his wife. So we swapped partners for future lessons and that worked well. I had a major hiccup with my first driving test though. A man talking to his friends stepped backwards into the road in front of me and made contact with the front wing of the car. I was flustered and drove on and of course failed the test. I learnt the hard way about the law stating you must stop after an accident.

The only other time I fell out with John was also driving-related. We had set off for our annual holiday, motoring down to Woolfardisworthy in Devon, when I failed to understand the Ordnance Survey map and got the directions wrong. Of course, John understood Ordnance Survey maps and all their tiny details but they are not useful for road trips. I made him stop the car and told him, 'I've never read a map in my life. You're the clever one, you've even plotted aircraft. You'll have to take over, and by the way I'm not one of your pupils.' The girls, overhearing this from the back of the car, were getting nervous. They had never heard John and me annoyed with each other. I'm happy to say their childhood was turning out much calmer and more peaceful than mine had been.

It's true that John was a perfectionist, but that was very useful. He would get upset about the wallpaper that wouldn't go on properly, or the flower-bed edging that wasn't perfectly straight. Once he changed places with me at the tea table because he couldn't stand the sight of the neighbours' washing line which wasn't quite straight. I teased him about it but there were advantages.

He loved the detail in everything. That was a huge plus when we were sightseeing on holiday. He could tell the girls all about the history of little towns we visited in Devon and Cornwall. We loved going back to the same tourist spots year after year, and the same guesthouse where they made us a picnic for days out and looked on us as part of the family. At Tintagel we visited the castle ruins and the girls were enchanted by John's tales of King Arthur, standing on the clifftop and looking out to sea where an imaginary Queen Guinevere was sailing away, flaming arrows being fired at her as she tried to escape. He taught Sandra and Carole how to surf in the big waves off Bude beach, and made kites for them to fly together.

On a holiday in Scarborough, on the Yorkshire coast, we took out rowing boats on a lake in Peasholm Park and I managed to get stuck, unable to turn round for the shore, with Sandra and I frantically trying to manage the oars. John and Carole were already back on shore, yelling at us with instructions. We were giggling helplessly and had to get a tow-in.

They were happy days, and both daughters still remember the rules, the boundaries, that kept it all together. They value the minor tellings-off and passed on the same family values to their children.

Sandra still remembers a significant incident at the age of 5 when she took a handful of toffees instead of the regulation single one, and had two smacks for it – one for 'lying' when she got caught, the other for 'stealing' more than one toffee. Small smacks but she remembers them to this day.

Years later, there was a bigger lesson to learn when Sandra and Carole were fighting in the back of the car as we set off for our annual holiday in the West Country. They had one or two warnings from John, then he simply turned the car round and headed back home. All the fun they had been looking forward to had suddenly turned sour; they were wide-eyed with the shock of the punishment.

Many hours later, after dark, we set off again with lilo beds in the back of the car. They could sleep all the way there, no fighting. That was another lesson they never forgot. They were learning about boundaries, the cornerstone of family life.

Today they admit they were useful lessons. Sandra recalls how her cousins always seemed to have more freedom when they were all small children. They ran wild, riding go-karts down the back of a row of shops, wading into stagnant water in the fields at the back of Rookery Lane, fishing out a dead cat. One of her cousins was trespassing in a cornfield, when the farmer's combine harvester all but ran him over. He was only slightly injured but it was a lesson. John and I were looked on as strict by comparison, but it was all about staying safe and being polite, and kind. We felt we'd managed to pull ourselves out of an earlier life overshadowed by the misery of war and poverty. We set ourselves some high standards and we did everything we could to get the girls to live by them.

Our city was enjoying a new beginning too. There was general agreement that Coventry was something of a phoenix, rising out of the ashes of a fire. A grand bronze statue was commissioned from local sculptor George Wagstaffe, showing a young person – instead of the traditional bird – symbolising the new city and its people rising out of wartime fire-bombing. It's a dramatic sight which we've come to love, unveiled in 1962 by Princess Margaret.

But I was feeling restless. The girls were at school all day, John was immersed in his teaching, and I needed to polish up my career skills again and contribute more to the household. I started looking for a job.

9

A Good Life, Well Lived

It seems extraordinary now but in the Sixties there was a great deal of debate about whether married women with children should go to work. It was almost as if we didn't have a free choice. In fact, until 1940 many employers sacked women when they became pregnant. There was no such thing as maternity pay and no job for a woman to come back to once she had her baby. Ironically, married women with children had been expected to work when the country needed them, yet they were frowned upon for seeking jobs once the war had ended.

In 1940, Ernest Bevin, the Minister of Labour, had set up day nurseries for women with children under school age so that they could work in the munitions factories. There were 1,500 of these wartime day nurseries in England during the Second World War where mothers paid 1s per day per child for care and food. Mothers had to supply the nappies. Working women who were breastfeeding were allowed breaks from their jobs every four hours to go to the nursery. The local authorities ran them, with the Ministry of Health providing funding.

By 1943, there had been 1½ million women working in essential industries like munitions and engineering. There were no part-time jobs. A woman would do a 10–12-hour shift just like the male workers. There was a forceful recruitment campaign throughout the war. But by the late Fifties and early Sixties it seemed a woman's place was once more supposed to be in the home. Young, unmarried women were beginning to go to university but there were few established careers for them beyond teaching, nursing or secretarial. For women like me with school-age children it was still the norm to stay at home, do the housework and care full-time for the family. There were government debates, newspaper and magazine articles and social surveys all devoted to moralising about working mothers. The starting point was always the fact that traditionally women had looked on work as a prelude to the real purpose of their lives – marriage and home-making.

Academic studies concluded that what women really wanted was a sense of usefulness, of contributing financially to the home and, just as important, they needed the social and mental stimulus of having a job and colleagues. Some sectors of the media argued that all children of school age needed the stability of having their mothers at home. The wartime day nurseries had by now closed down and any childcare outside the home would be either expensive or a burden on close relatives. While this was becoming the raging debate of the day, I had already decided that I wanted and needed to find a job.

Our house needed more furniture and the garden had not even been fenced or dug over. I wanted to contribute. With my experience and skills, I felt sure I could find a well-paid job that would make the difference to our finances. And my daily life would become more rewarding. John and I solved the question of childcare when he went to night shifts to study for his teaching degree. He would earn more, work only four nights a week, and would be there to see the girls off to school and welcome them back at the end of the day. I found an administrative job at Courtaulds, the huge textile company employing thousands at its works in Foleshill. I was happy to be working on schedules, monitoring the arrival of machine parts as they came in and chasing up all the paperwork.

I loved the busy atmosphere, the friendly faces and the smooth-running office. It was a pleasant contrast to the strictness at the Co-op insurance office where there had been a no-talking rule and a bossy manager. I was finding my way round the entire factory, checking on deliveries and getting to know everyone from the managers to the shop-floor workers. But after a while I began to develop a terrible rash on my face and arms. Hospital tests tracked it down to the chemicals in the paper I was using all day. I had to hand in my notice.

The manager of Courtaulds site services told me I shouldn't leave. His secretary was having a baby and she wouldn't be coming back. He wanted me to have her job. I transferred to his department and found myself with a full-time responsible job I learned to love. I spent twenty-two years there and ended up feeling like part of the institution itself. Today I still meet up for coffee mornings with our group, 'the Courtaulds' ladies', and chat about the old days.

My job was quite a responsibility, I did the minutes of meetings and all the administration for our departments. Site services covered the factory's transport requirements and all safety matters. Tens of thousands of people worked there and the car park held hundreds of vehicles. The works stretched down two sides of Foleshill Road, with the engineering side going all the way to Stoney Stanton Road and the other side housing the textile mills. We made fabrics for household goods and were in the forefront of the production of man-made materials like crimplene, nylon and terylene. One of my department's responsibilities was the safety issues for heavy gangs moving machinery around the factory. Hydraulics were not sophisticated like they are today and there were some sad incidents where men were crushed. I saw one of these terrible accidents myself as a gang was bringing in a huge metal safe. It was too big for the doorway and during the wait for carpenters to dismantle the doorframe a supervisor, George, whom I knew and liked, somehow took the full force when the safe fell. These incidents had to be investigated and recorded in great detail; it was a part of my job that I dreaded. One morning I was called into work early by my boss who had already been there nearly all night, organising the aftermath of a terrible thunderstorm. The entire spinneret department, where dozens of extrusion machines operated twenty-four hours round the clock to produce fibres, was flooded. I saw that my boss had rolled his sleeves up and put on his wellies to work with the men. He needed me to organise breakfast in the canteen for them. An hour later they were tucking into bacon, eggs, sausage and beans.

I liked the way that Courtaulds looked after its employees. The factory had been built on a canalside, and there were landscaped gardens around the entire works. Many of us used to bring our packed lunches to the grassy banks of the canal and watch the swans. Courtaulds was an industry leader in Coventry, becoming the world's main producer of man-made fibres like rayon and nylon. Built up since the eighteenth century as an important centre of silk-weaving, it had turned to making parachutes during the Second World War.

Wartime brides had made their dresses from Courtaulds' parachute silk. There was a benevolent ethos towards its workers, offering them a full social life in the interests of camaraderie and good morale. The factory had its own cricket ground and a competitive team, as well as a football pitch and other sports clubs which welcomed workers and their families.

It provided a nightlife too, with a social club organising dinner dances every weekend. It was good to get to know our co-workers. A big draw to the social club was that drinks were heavily subsidised by the company and cost next to nothing. John and I often went to the dances, glamorous affairs where the women were in long dresses and the men in smart suits with white shirts. We had a six- or seven-piece band playing swing numbers and all the latest dance rhythms and of course there were all-important wartime songs we

loved. Our girls Sandra and Carole would be safely in bed
at their grandparents' house so we could relax. John and I
were keen on the quickstep and the waltz. He drank very
little and was always so gentlemanly. I remember a couple
of show-offs who liked to take over the dance floor, exag-
gerating all their moves. The woman slipped and fell during
an exotic tango, and slid from one end of the dance floor to
the other. There was laughing and clapping from most of
the crowd, but my John moved in quickly to help her up.

He had the perfect manners, instilled in him by his parents
and the Royal Navy. He loved his time in the Fleet Air Arm,
respecting all the discipline, the spotless uniforms and the
endless rules and regulations. He told me how he once walked
across an area of the deck which was off limits, apparently a
grave breach of the rules, and was yelled at by Prince Philip,
by then the Duke of Edinburgh, himself a devout Navy man,
who was visiting John's training ship at the time.

He loved his two years of national service and would have
liked to join up as a regular in the Royal Navy. But there was
his apprenticeship, and our marriage, to consider. Happily,
he chose us.

John and I got on so well, we shared the work of running the home and family equally. I cooked and did the
housework, but he was a wizard at DIY and our car never
once needed to go to a garage. John organised the garage so
that all his tools were neatly at hand and always clean and
ready for use. Over the years we had a Triumph Herald, a
Morris Oxford and a Ford Cortina estate. A red sporty VW
Scirocco was one of his favourites, but he found it difficult
to get in and out of so part-exchanged it for a white Audi

saloon, his pride and joy. He planned the garden so it became a haven for the girls and provided colour and sanctuary all year round. The shed was concealed by a pretty pergola where he made a swing for Sandra and Carole, and there was a path running beside the lawn to keep us off his precious grass, and a rustic bench on some hard-standing at the back, under the apple tree.

John planted the Bramley tree as a sapling and it continues to produce beautiful flowers in spring, a nesting-place for visiting birds and a natural climbing frame for my grandchildren. We sent away for a wisteria, knowing that the little seedling would not flower for several years. John nurtured it and trained it up the side of the pergola, and was furious when it produced white flowers instead of the traditional blue. He complained to the nursery and found it was their mistake, but we came to love the scented blooms that still trail across the entire pergola in spring and early summer.

Thanks to my job we could now afford to stock the garden nicely, and indoors we had a television and household aids like a twintub washing machine, a far cry from the old copper tub my mother had used. The neighbourhood was busy and friendly. We often got together for suppers and drinks. I would cook and John would prepare the extended table in the dining room. It was so easy to visit each other's homes, just a walk away. At New Year we would often draw up a plan to celebrate in each other's homes, with food and drinks in one house, music and dancing in another, and the chimes of midnight in another. Families would bring home-made beer and elderberry wine.

John's sister Eileen had married a New Zealander and decided to move there at a time when many British families were thinking about a new life there or in Australia or South Africa, or Canada. Britain's post-war period was austere and there was a promise of a new life and new beginning overseas which made the move seem tempting. But not for us. John's parents were planning to join his sister and her family in New Zealand and of course we talked about the possibilities. Sadly, his dad died before they could make the move.

But we were both English to the core and couldn't imagine a life anywhere else. We were Coventry born and bred and shared a strong connection to the city and its fortunes. We were proud of its great contribution to the war effort and its growing reputation as a model of peace and reconciliation. It helped us make some sort of sense out of the horrors of the Blitz.

John and I, despite our contrasting political views, shared a great admiration for Churchill and all our war leaders. Several times we went to London to be at the Royal Albert Hall for the Last Night of the Proms with all its patriotic songs and fervour. We used to make a weekend of it so we could see Buckingham Palace and the other great sights. John was a Labour Party man through and through and I was staunchly Conservative but, amazingly, it never led to rows. He was a great champion of workers' rights and would always support a fight for justice. Of course, I believed in fairness too, though it could be testing when trade unions became active in Coventry's many manufacturing industries.

I recall only one strike at Courtaulds, and it lasted for just a day in April 1970. Two hundred workers came out to support a controversial wage claim and my boss and I had to face a picket line. There was no trouble, we were relieved to find, as the men knew and respected our department for its important role in their safety and security. They let us through without any problems.

A family of four was our dream. Neither of us wanted a big chaotic household where there wasn't enough to go round, or enough time or space for the children to be listened to. The result was a happy home where kindness ruled. John believed in discipline but it was meted out with kindness. If the girls were arguing, he would make them come to him and explain the cause. Each girl would have a turn to speak. He would tell them solemnly to make up, however trivial the falling-out. He would not tolerate sulky or grumpy behaviour. That rubbed off on me too. If there was a minor problem and a few grumpy words from me, he would walk up to the end of the garden and look at his trees and shrubs. In due course he would return and put his arm round me. 'All right now, luv?' he would say. That's all it took. He was a lovable presence in the house and the girls and I were very sympathetic, and worried about him, when he suffered migraines. He was so susceptible to that terrible blinding pain that he would avoid trigger foods like cheese or chocolate, and certain noises. When he was developing a migraine the mere rustling of clothes caused him actual pain. He would close his eyes and try to rest in an armchair. I would heat some towels and put them around his neck for some small comfort.

We never knew the cause and I know many people suffer like John. During a very bad attack he would go upstairs and lie in a darkened room, hurting too much to move or speak. He would patiently see it through, sometimes for many hours, without complaint. He was calm and quiet, rarely bad-tempered about anything.

He would get irritated though if DIY projects didn't go exactly to plan or something in the house wasn't in its right place. One day he was helping to clear the table, carrying dishes out to the kitchen, and we heard him go flying with a great crash as he slipped on a rug on the polished parquet in the hallway. The rug was crunched up and hurled through the window into the garden with much muttering and abuse. Carole rushed to help him, full of concern, while Sandra and I collapsed with the giggles in the sitting room.

It became complicated during the school holidays when John went back to working daytime hours, so I made an arrangement with my sister Rosie, paying her to have the girls while I was at Courtaulds.

They loved playing with her children and it was helpful for me to be able to drop them off and collect them later, knowing they were safe and cared for. Later, after my parents retired they would sometimes have the children. My dad, restless to the end, didn't want to just stay at home. He had sold up his small business interests and retired at 60 but he still had a lot of energy. He and my mum both took jobs managing the Green Room at the Belgrade Theatre in the city centre, with Dad helping to build scenery for the repertory company and taking charge of the stage door. I could drop Carole off at the theatre for a while on Saturday mornings while I went shopping, and both Sandra and Carole loved to spend time there with them, exploring behind the scenes and meeting the actors. My dad had mellowed in later life and it was a revelation to see him smiling and playing with his granddaughters, treating them with a kindness I had never experienced from him as a child.

I remember how shocked I was when we all watched the Remembrance Sunday service on television together and saw my father shed tears. Under the harsh, stern exterior that blighted my childhood he clearly had sad, searing memories of those terrible years at Ypres.

He and my mum became doting grandparents and it worked out well; there we were after the chaos of my childhood, a successful extended family who continued to live locally and see a lot of each other.

I sometimes felt my sisters and their families looked on me as overly ambitious. It's true that I was the only one who had followed a career beyond getting married. My closest sister Anne had trained as a nurse but she gave that up, as so many women did, once she had a family and that meant that money continued to be short.

But I had found everything I had dreamed of all my young life. From my earliest years I knew there was a better, happier way to be and through John and our life together I was now living it. There is nothing wrong in wanting to work towards a goal, and you can definitely achieve it if you want it desperately enough, whatever the challenge. I saw that my parents were still living a disordered life, even a little bit squalid. Dad would sit by the fire with a hacking cough, smoking his Woodbines, and Mum's kitchen was always full of empty, grubby milk bottles and stacks of yellowing old newspapers. My girls would ask me about it, but we said nothing to my parents. My dad was suffering from emphysema and bronchitis, the legacy of years working with coal and living through the polluted fog that came from Coventry's many factories before the clean air legislation. He died at 65 and my sister Irene and her family moved in to care for my mum. I was relieved that my mum's later years were comfortable and companionable. She had been my only protector during the rough early years.

When both parents had gone, and we had buried my mum with a great deal of sorrow, there was just the proceeds of their small house to share. All those years of back-breaking work by my father had only managed to get him and his seven children through the war years. For all his astute investments in terraced houses and shops in Coventry, there was little to show. Property wealth was unknown during the war and subsequent years. I've always been glad that I started out with nothing; it's made me appreciate the good things that come along with hard work and ambition and the keen desire to make a comfortable home. John and I wished for nothing more than our home and garden; we never even considered moving. Sandra and Carole had grown up there and made many friends with our near neighbours. They had brought boyfriends home over the years and we'd had many jolly parties. Both of them did well and pursued careers. When they got married, we naturally planned it all from home and held the wedding services at St James, the parish church where we'd attended every Sunday as a family.

Once they were leading independent lives, we began to take longer holidays, several times going abroad with friends. John had six weeks off every summer in line with his college students' holidays, so we were able to plan visits to his sister Eileen and her family now living in New Zealand. Most of our trips had been to France or Austria, short distances away. We had driven to France many times, once memorably visiting the war graves at Normandy. We both found it traumatic and heartbreaking, all those teenage soldiers buried, but we were glad we had made the journey there to pray and pay tribute to them. We had personally suffered a great deal from both world wars, but these men had paid a much higher price and their families would never recover.

In late summer 1985, we decided on another trip to New Zealand. Eileen was John's only sibling and they were very close. It was important to spend time with her. We were happy to make it to her son Ian's wedding in the August. We made many plans for a few years ahead when John would retire at 60. We would take more holidays and enjoy the freedom of it all. But during those last few days in New Zealand John said he felt unwell. We decided he should see the doctor on our return home.

One morning he decided to go in late to work, as he didn't feel well at all. We called the family doctor and he came to the house to do some basic tests. He diagnosed angina and told John he would have to take life a little easier. He gave me a prescription for tablets to pop under the tongue. I set off for the chemist and by the time I came home John was feeling worse. He had gone upstairs to lie down. Within minutes he had died. I was frantic, flying downstairs in a panic and out into the road to get help.

A kind man passing by, a complete stranger, said he was a first-aider and came in to see John. I'll never forget him coming downstairs just a few minutes later to tell me, 'I'm sorry luv, he's gone.' He was only 56 and we'd believed we had many more happy years ahead of us.

I was in such deep shock that I couldn't speak properly for several days. I would try to say the words but they just wouldn't come. I have never needed my family more than at that time and they were marvellous, patient and comforting. They dealt with all the many arrangements and paperwork that needed to be done. Sandra and Carole stayed at my side throughout and somehow it was Carole's son Andrew, my little grandson, who turned out to be one of my greatest comforts. Children can't take in the enormity of death, of course, and they continue to have their needs so you have to tend to them. The simple necessity of caring for him and sharing childlike conversations helped me get back to something like normality.

I missed John every moment and all these years later I still do. He's everywhere around me, in the garden he grew and loved and the house where he did all the painting and decorating and planning. We had done everything together for thirty-five years, sharing the chores like banking and shopping and enjoying our daughters and grandchildren. It wasn't fair and I struggled with that, at the same time turning to God and my beliefs to help me get through. I was always a regular churchgoer and I found that a great comfort when John died. I joined a church group and that helped in a small way to plan my week and try to see ahead to a life without him.

I was lucky in that my family was always on hand. They were grieving themselves but still took on the essential tasks which I couldn't face. Our solicitor told me that John's life insurance meant the mortgage on the house would be paid off. Important milestones like that made things a little easier, but it took years to accept he was gone and with him all the love and hope we had shared.

Meeting John and loving him had changed my life from misery and chaos to happiness and peace. That's how much we meant to each other. I can't advise others about how to deal with the huge burden of bereavement, but I know that eventually, with prayers, acceptance and the solid presence of family and friends, I've got through it and arrived at a calm, happy place. It's hard to think that I have now spent as many years without John as I did with him. Of course, he lives on in my daughters and grandchildren and we speak about him often.

I tried to rebuild the routine of my life when he died. Sandra and Carole reminded me that I was strong and resilient and we did more together. I joined a gym and made new friends and I had plenty of time on my hands to help with the grandchildren. I was still only in my late fifties and had good friends to share holidays and outings with. Once I splashed out on a skiing trip to Switzerland with a group of friends. I did my best but by the end of day one I had already embarrassed myself. The handsome ski instructor told me, 'Mabel, parallel your skis! Parallel!' I did exactly as I was told and was launched at speed down the slope in front of me. As I crash-landed at the bottom the instructor was waiting for me. I fell into his arms and hung on there for dear life, to the great delight of onlookers. I never lived that down.

The girls were marvellous and made sure I was never really lonely. As I've got older our roles have reversed quite naturally. They look after me as attentively as I once looked after them. It was Carole who first noticed I looked unwell. At the age of 80 I was still feeling healthy and energetic, doing my own housework and cooking. But something was clearly wrong. One day I noticed blood in my urine and we knew that could be serious. I went to the Walsgrave Hospital, now called the Coventry University Hospital, and it was comforting that one of my nieces, Polly, was a nurse there and able to take a personal interest in my case. I was diagnosed with bladder cancer and told that it was serious. They had found several tumours.

I feel I was one of the lucky ones because I was offered a chance to take part in some new drugs trials and that would mean I didn't need surgery or chemotherapy. The specialists were taking an interest because they wanted to investigate any possible link to my work at Courtaulds where many chemicals were being used.

There was a meeting where I consented to medical students being present, and I was asked if I would do clinical trials. I looked at them and thought how important it was that they should become doctors. I felt I should take part for their sakes. The trials meant regular check-ups, and bladder wash-outs where a solution was introduced by catheter. It would mean I felt quite ill for a few days afterwards. It was an alternative to chemotherapy so there were advantages, but I came to dread those sessions.

The treatment was immediately followed by feeling cold and shivery and unwell. I continued until the sessions became six-monthly then yearly. Around my ninetieth birthday they called me in for a further session but I decided I had had enough. I felt I had done my duty as a good citizen and also I was feeling well and happy in the knowledge that we had shrunk the tumours and beaten the cancer. I had been under-going treatment for ten years, enough was enough.

And to take my mind off all that there were family plans for a ninetieth birthday party.

All our friends and neighbours came for tea in the garden with scones and cream and a birthday cake, catered by me and my daughters. It was a happy day and there was more to come.

My grandson Matt took me down to London in grand style for a surprise celebration at The Ritz. I cherish the memory of a glamorous party, a concert pianist playing throughout, and all my family around me as I cut my birthday cake. We stayed overnight in adjoining rooms at Brown's Hotel and shared a luxury room-service breakfast in the morning.

I'm so proud of my daughters and my grandchildren, all of them great achievers. After my own childhood of pov-erty, lacking education and encouragement, I never dreamed I could be so lucky.

I've seen sorrow in my life, but also love and happiness. Today I can say, hand on heart, I am feeling very blessed.

My Proud Legacy

In my own quiet way, I feel I have achieved a good life with many rewards that help to cancel out the painful early years. At 93 I feel happy and at peace with myself and all around me. A loving family and friends mean a great deal and they are kind enough to say I'm something of a role model when it comes to dealing with adversity and emerging with contentment.

My daughters Sandra and Carole still look to me for guidance and we've made a smooth transition which means they are now caring for me when it comes to shopping and housework. I still cherish my independence but they and my lovely grandchildren are always on hand. They seem to enjoy my company and all my stories from our shared family history. I never know a moment of loneliness and I'm aware that is a blessing in older age.

When our clan of four generations including my four grandchildren and five great-grandchildren get together, they make me feel like the star of the show and of course I enjoy that. They know I've been through very tough times and seem to listen when I remind them about the need for peace and kindness in their lives.

Over the years, I've passed down some wise old sayings that my own mother lived by:

'It's always darkest just before dawn – things will be okay.'
'To err is human, to forgive divine.'
'Don't judge others lest you yourself be judged.'
'If a job is worth doing, it's worth doing well.'
'Be nice to people on the way up, you might meet them again on the way down.'
'Do as you would be done by.'
'You have to be a friend to have a friend.'
'Let it out, a good cry does you the world of good.'

I try to pass on my love of our country too and always remind the family how lucky they are to have been born here and to have enjoyed peace in their lifetime. I live by a strong belief in respect, kindness and love and I hope they will too.

A few years ago, my grandson Matt and I were talking about how to combine ambition in the business world with a practical show of compassion to others less fortunate. He and I have always been moved by the plight of children living in poverty; we've both wept at the back stories told during the BBC's annual Children in Need fundraising efforts. Now we discussed what we might actually achieve if we worked together. Matt told me, 'There's a lot of love in our family and we are financially secure. Surely, we can find a project that can be both commercially viable and help underprivileged children. It can be a challenge but also fun, and it will be your proud legacy, I'll make sure of that.'

So that's how Mabel's Enterprise was born, a competitive but honest and truly social business that would raise funds from which every penny would go to our favourite cause: the enrichment of children's lives. Matt's background is in the successful corporate world and he has given that up willingly to work full-time for Mabel's Enterprise instead. It is not a registered charity; it's a community interest company which measures its success by its impact on local communities. There are currently no paid staff and there will never be shareholders. Matt and I work for free and every penny we raise goes to projects for children living in poverty.

Matt is the brains behind it. He's developed two sides: Mabel's Business and Mabel's Fund. All the profits we make from the business are channelled into the fund. We have co-authored a picture-book series for children and produced an organic clothing range for children. Together with the proceeds from this book, all funds will go to projects to enhance the lives of some of the country's poorest children.

We looked at some shocking statistics which show the stark facts about child poverty in Britain. We examined reports published by the government's Children's Commissioner and by the End Child Poverty Coalition. The figures they gave were for 2019/20 when 31 per cent of children in the UK were living below the poverty line, and the situation has worsened since then. I could hardly believe that more than 1.1 million children live in workless families; more than a million children suffer with emotional or mental health issues; nearly a million children are or have been neglected; more than 800,000 children are regularly bullied; and nearly 125,000 children live in temporary housing.

According to the Child Poverty Action Group, the definition of child poverty is living in a household where the income is 60 per cent less than the national average and the family cannot adequately heat their home, pay their rent or buy essentials for their children. The group says: 'A child can have three meals a day, warm clothes and go to school but still be poor because his or her parents don't have enough money to ensure they can live in a warm home, have access to a computer for their homework, or go on the same school trips as their classmates.'

Matt and I found our inspiration right there. The school trips, which are inspiring and educational, bringing purpose to young lives and often uncovering hidden talents and skills, could be funded by us with the collaboration of schools in the most-needy areas. We've set ourselves an objective of funding 2 million school trips by 2030.

We identified one of the highest areas of child poverty in Birmingham, the Hodge Hill constituency, where there is a distressing 57 per cent child poverty rate – the fifth worst rate nationally. The largest school is Washwood Heath Academy with more than 1,700 pupils, from reception class to Year 13. Matt had talks with the head of Primary Phase, and asked her to identify problem areas of funding. She immediately flagged up extra-curricular trips as a real challenge. They had not been able to offer these since 2013 because local families simply could not afford to pay for them. Despite teachers doing a great job in enriching children's learning in school and at after-school clubs, often partly funded by the staff themselves, the children were missing out on trips.

The school is rated Good by Ofsted so we know it performs well. Matt and I were upset to learn of the problems. We had read many studies which conclude that extra-curricular programmes stimulate good school attendance and mental health and improve academic performance. The government's own Social Mobility Commission report in July 2019 concludes that these programmes foster friendships and improve resilience and confidence. They build softer life skills which impact both home and work. We could see a way to contribute to this great resource, starting with Washwood Heath Academy. We could help to provide those 'inspiration moments' for children, uncovering their hidden talents, keeping them off the streets and bringing some purpose to them. The long-term effect can reduce crime and increase employment. It can make the world a better place.

So we fully funded some trips in June and October 2021, taking the entire primary school of 210 pupils to:

Reception class – Ash End Farm
Years 1 and 2 – Conkers Outdoor Adventure
Year 3 – The Black Country Living Museum
Year 4 – The National Space Centre
Year 5 – Go Ape
Year 6 – The Challenge Academy, Baggeridge

In April 2021, we provided a £3,700 subsidy for Year 7's three-day residential stay at PGL Boreatton Park outdoor adventure centre in Shrewsbury. Using the proceeds of our sales from books and clothing, we brought the cost of the trip down from £141 to around £70 per pupil. This trip simply couldn't have happened without our subsidy.

It's been my great pleasure to be able to talk about these schemes and our vision in several radio and local TV appearances and I hope to soon be able to speak to students at Washwood Heath Academy. You might think that young people consider the lived experience of wartime by those of my age to be as uninteresting as ancient history, but all of them have now, sadly, seen the brutality of war in all its horrific detail on their TV screens during Russia's cruel invasion of Ukraine. They have wept at footage of mothers and children trapped in dark, airless cellars, helpless as they listen to continual bombardment of their homes. Who better to tell them gently that yes, this happened here in our country during my lifetime and we must work together to ensure it must not happen again?

I also hope to read to them from our innovative series of picture books. Matt has created the Tingalings, five lovable characters who promote kindness and climate change awareness. With beautiful illustrations he brings Braveling, Sparkling, Darling, Smartling and Bumbling into adventures one character at a time, to open young eyes to climate change's extensive reach, with easy ideas about reducing our carbon output at home.

We have already published four titles stocked at Waterstones and other high-street retailers: *Darling Saves a Koala*; *Braveling Saves a Snow Leopard*; *Smartling Saves a Sea Turtle*; and *Sparkling Saves a Tiger*. All are printed in the UK on recycled paper. Tingalings hoodies, jumpers and T-shirts are all printed in the UK, on demand, using organic cotton.

To date, we have sold more than 1,500 copies via online sales, local markets and fundraising, and corporate partnerships. In doing so we have also free-issued over 1,800 copies to good causes, including Home-Start, Birmingham – a fantastic charity supporting families with children facing difficult life circumstances. We have been shocked to discover that more than 14,000 children in Birmingham do not have a book of their own.

In the pipeline is a Tingalings TV series. Matt is working on a children's TV show proposal and script with an award-winning scriptwriter and will be pitching to broadcasters and production companies. I can help with this by promoting the books on local TV and radio.

Matt and I feel passionately about our business model, offering quality children's products and services and at the same time offering the opportunity to help children less fortunate. This is a unique market offer that gives us a good competitive advantage going forward, driven by impact and not shareholders. We want to expand into further children's books, clothes, TV animations, educational resources and local meeting places such as coffee shops and play centres.

Matt is confident that Mabel's Enterprise will live on beyond my years and we agree there is no better life purpose than investing in the next generation. I'm so proud the business carries my name and will be my legacy.

You can contribute to our efforts by making purchases at our online shop at www.tingalings.co.uk or by clicking on the link on our website, www.mabelsenterprise.com.

Mabel's Enterprise

All author proceeds from the sale of this book are transferred to Mabel's Fund to pay for future school trips. Thank you for making a difference to children's lives.

Love, Mabel